History of Handkerchiefs

Each year, I always gave my piano teacher, Mrs Trimble, a hanky as a special gift.

Fran Techlow
1954

Before Kleenex and Puffs tissues, hankies were a vital item. Every gentleman had a hankie in his pocket, and every lady carried one in her sleeve or purse.

The containers above are vintage hankie holders. As you can see, some were very ornate. These beautiful boxes and wrappers were appreciated as much as the embroidered hankies they held.

Collectible handkerchief holders can be store bought or handmade in character. In vintage times a box of hankies was considered the perfect gift and all styles, designs and colors of hankies were available in dry goods stores.

Hankies were also available in handmade boxes such as these Victorian era containers that are exquisitely decorated with handmade tatting, lace, embroidery, bark, seashells and nature's materials.

I love old trunks. One day I discovered a reasonably priced old doll trunk at an antique store. Although there was no doll inside, it was filled with hand-sewn doll clothes.

In addition to skirts, blouses, dresses and hats there were several aprons. Every apron had a tiny handkerchief, which was about the size of a dime. Precious!

Janet Carruth

Redwork Fruit Table Runner

Redwork embroidered fruit make the perfect complement for the colors in these handkerchiefs.

It's the unusual color choice of the hankies that makes this project so striking. We found a group of matching hankies on ebay and filled in with a few from our own collection that blended.

Instructions on page 25
Patterns on pages 26-29

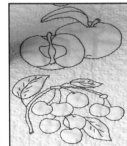

Amy's Adventures

This quilt is a wonderful way to use those lovely flowered handkerchiefs that have a decorative edge!

This sweet young lady doesn't let any grass grow under her feet! She keeps busy, busy, busy doing all the things a proper young lady should- piano practice, dancing, and picking flowers. Outdoors, she feeds the birds and chickens, plays with the dog, and picks apples. She spends her spare time jumping rope and looking wistfully out the window.

Perfect for your daughter's room or a very feminine guest room, this pretty quilt brings a bit of nostalgic elegance to any room.

Instructions on page 30-31 • Patterns on pages 32-44

May Baskets

I n many parts of the country it is a custom for children to make paper baskets for May Day. These fragile gifts were filled with flowers and hung on the doorknobs of friends. The excitement came when one tried not to get caught leaving these pretty offerings. Ring the doorbell and run away! Will the deliverer get caught?

These baskets and flowers won't dim with time and you'll want everyone to find out you are the maker.

Instructions on page 45-46 • Patterns on pages 47-55

Those Adorable Waitresses

This quilt honors those hard-working ladies of the 40's and 50's who wore heavily starched, mostly solid colored uniforms enhanced only by a large hanky placed in their left breast pocket. The hanky, which was the only way each woman expressed her own individuality, was a sight to see. Every hanky was different, but all were starched and elaborately folded or arranged in a unique one-of-a-kind way. Was there status to the way each chose to display hers? I've become intrigued about these hanky-wearing women. This project provides a perfect spot for those handkerchiefs that are too beautiful or too sentimental to cut up.

Please contact me (www.hanky@irughook.com) if you have stories, photos or perhaps even an intricately folded hanky worn by one of these women.

Instructions on page 56 • Patterns on page 57

Nursery Time Cuties

Soft, delicate and pretty, these nursery necessities are a welcome departure from the usual teddy bear motif. This set includes crib bumper pads, a diaper bag, flannel quilt, and tooth fairy pillow.

Instructions on pages 58 - 61

Magic Hanky... Baby Bonnet

I'm just a little hanky,
As square as square can be,
But with a few stitches,
They made a bonnet out of me.
I'll be worn home from the
 hospital,
Or on the christening day,
Then I'll be carefully pressed
And neatly put away.
For her wedding day,
As we have all been told,
Every well-dressed bride must wear
Something that is old.
What would be more fitting
Than to find little me,
A few stitches snipped,
A wedding hanky I will be.
And if perchance it is a boy,
Someday he'll surely wed,
So to his bride he can present
This hanky he once wore
 on his head.

Author Unknown

Baby Bonnets

Perfect for a Princess

A simple, wonderfully easy bonnet for a precious babe. This has the added benefit of being easily converted to a bridal handkerchief when "the baby" too quickly becomes "the bride".

Do you wonder what every new-born princess should wear to her christening or blessing ceremony? This absolutely beautiful gown is so special that it will surely become an heirloom for future generations.

Instructions on page 62-63

Blue Work Kids

J ack and Jill went up the hill and Little Bo Peep is still looking for her sheep. Mary's flower garden seems to be growing well on this delightful Mother Goose set of embroideries. Place this little wall hanging in your child's room or on the wall next to the "story-time chair".

Instructions on page 64 • Patterns on pages 64-67

Curtain · Wreath · Pillow · Towel

Are you celebrating a marriage, anniversary, or Valentines Day? If so, hang up this heart pillow and put notes to your beloved in the pocket. Or, fill the pocket with silk roses for a bit of romance on your special day.

Redwork tea towels are always beautiful, no matter what design you choose. Our bird sings happily perched upon a branch. Let him bring a springtime song to your kitchen or bath.

Next time you need to soften the look of a space, consider a handkerchief curtain or wreath. Light and airy, these hankies give a lift to any space.

Wreath and Curtain instructions on page 70 · Pillow instructions on pages 68-69
Tea Towel instructions and pattern on page 71

Lampshade · Pillows Galore

Soft pastel coordinating prints complement the delicate lace butterfly edging on these envelope pillows. This is a frilly, feminine design that is sure to please your favorite princess. For those who enjoy embroidery, the flower pattern is a perfect project for teaching the next generation of stitchers. Create a memory that will last a lifetime when you share these wonderful designs with your daughter, granddaughter or niece. These projects make pretty Mother's Day gifts too! And for fans of hot glue, don't overlook the soft lampshade decorated with pretty hankies. This is a truly simple-to-do home dec idea.

Instructions on pages 72-74 · Patterns on pages 72-73

Perfect for a nursery or young child's room, these fun pillows come in bright colors and motifs that will stir the imagination. When you have a hanky with a white center and a printed border, the little train design is just the right size to fill that space.

Pom-pom fringe, rickrack and ribbon add texture and color to these fun accents.

I hope this collection inspires you to look at those unusual printed hankies with new eyes and try some bold color combinations.

Instructions and patterns on pages 74-75

Under the Big Top

What child does not sometimes dream of running away with the circus? It's so exciting - the lions, the elephants, and the camels are all waiting to be tamed, trained, or ridden. And that big top is just so colorful. The clowns run around making us all laugh while performers attempt daring feats of agility on the high wire and trapeze.

Let this wall hanging call out that inner child and escort your grown-up, far too busy mind back to a simpler time when dreams were possible and clouds became cotton candy with a moment's wishing.

Instructions on pages 76 • Patterns on pages 76-79

Fancy Framed Hanky & Tray

Special handkerchiefs deserve special framing. The stenciled leaf is the perfect complement for this beautiful handkerchief.

Want a tidy, tasteful, trendy, treasure? Try this terrific tray. I found a fabulous vintage hanky, but the hem was tattered, so I sewed a narrow picot ribbon to cover it.

It's a good idea to make friends with your neighborhood framer. This project is much easier if you can charm the framer into finishing the assembly for you!

Instructions and pattern on pages 80-81

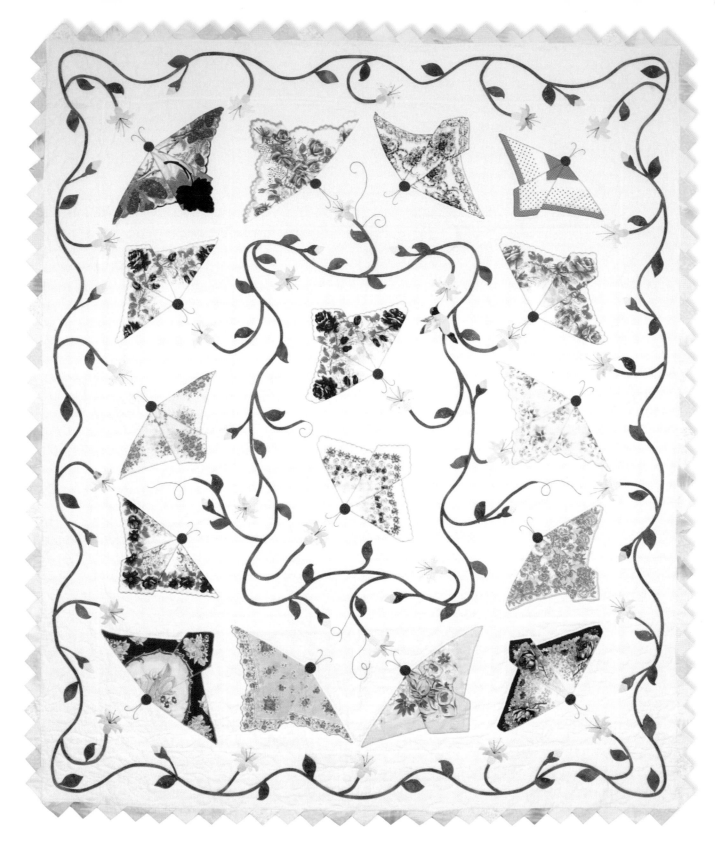

Butterfly Garden

Your heart is going to flutter when you make this dazzling quilt with its lily vine and yellow prairie point border. Delicate hankies form the wings of fluttering friends. You are going to love showing this quilt to family and friends. Bring a fresh spring breeze into any room with this amazing masterpiece.

Instructions and patterns on page 82 - 89

Chenille Throw

I rresistibly soft, this cozy throw is pretty enough to leave out on the sofa, or put in the guest room; friends will surely feel welcome.

We used a vintage chenille bedspread. We cut squares from the center and cut off the fringe to use for the trim. However, you can purchase wonderful chenille fabric and trim-by-the-yard.

Instructions on page 90

Pincushion

W ouldn't these sachets make the cutest bride's gift to helpers at her wedding? She'll be able to make many because they go so fast. This is also a perfect project for small handkerchiefs.

Hanky Babies

O ften made for church or other times when children need a quiet toy, these hanky babies are so pretty and easy to make. You'll keep as well as give these sweet little babies.

Instructions on page 91

A Lovely Blue Basket

I love handwork because it is very calming. I especially love embroidery because my great grandmother taught me how to do it when I was only four years old. A hand stitcher's delight, this wall hanging allows you to practice your needle turn applique in the center block and show off your embroidery skills with the stem stitched flowers in the triangles. The hand-quilting in the center is cross-hatched every inch, with simple straight line quilting in the triangles.

Delicate yellow handkerchiefs with lovely edges form the border around this simply beautiful flower basket. If you can't find a variety of yellow handkerchiefs, dye some white ones with Rit.

Instructions on page 19 · Patterns on pages 19-24

Please Note:

Applique and embroidery cause fabric to draw up a little. Most of our instructions specify cutting these shapes larger than needed; then after the applique or embroidery is complete, trimming to the correct size.

All seams in this book are ¼" unless otherwise noted. Some of the binding instructions in this book call for a ⅜" seam because the foot on my machine just happens to be ⅜". If you prefer a ¼" seam, use your ¼" foot.

FINISHED SIZE: 33" x 33"

FABRICS:

7 Yellow handkerchiefs (We overdyed some hankies with *Rit* dye to get enough.)
1 yard Tan for center square and triangles
¾ yard Blue for basket, sashing, borders and binding
1 yard pretty print for the backing
4" squares for applique flowers and leaves: 1 Red, 2 Yellow, 1 Green

MATERIALS:

Embroidery floss to match Blue fabric
Embroidery needle size 8
Applique needle size 11 sharp
Matching thread for applique
Batting

CUTTING:

1 Tan 17" square for the center
2 Tan 15" squares for embroidered flowers
1 Blue rectangle 6" x 10½" for basket applique
2 Blue 2½" x 16" strips for sashing
2 Blue 2½" x 20" strips for sashing
2 Blue 1⅛" x 23" strips cut on the bias for basket handles
2 Blue 3" x 28" strips for outer border
2 Blue 3" x 33" strips for outer border
3 Blue 2½" strips sewn together to make 136" for binding

INSTRUCTIONS:

1. Trace the basket, flower and leaf patterns onto the appropriate colored fabrics. Add a ³⁄₁₆" seam allowance around all the edges. Cut out the applique pieces. Fold the Blue basket handle fabric into thirds making it ⅜" and baste it down the middle. Pin all the applique pieces onto the center Tan square and sew each in place using the needle turn stitch. Press. Trim square to 16" x 16".

2. Cut 28 handkerchief corners using the triangle pattern for sashing embellishment. Place 7 Handkerchief corners along one edge of the appliqued center square right sides together. Pin. Place one Blue 2½" x 16" sashing strip over triangles right sides together. Pin and sew. Repeat for the opposite side. Press. Repeat for the other two sides using 2½" x 20" strips.

3. Press both Tan 15" squares in half diagonally. Following the Basic How-Tos on page 99, draw embroidery designs onto each triangle section. Draw two tulip patterns on one square and two open-faced flower patterns on the other square. Refer to diagram for placement. Embroider flowers using two strands of floss. Cut squares apart on the diagonal fold making four triangles. Trim the triangles to match the size of the sashing. You are matching the diagonal edge with the sashing. The square should be about 14¼".

4. Pin and sew one embroidered triangle onto one side of Blue sashing. Repeat on the opposite side. Press. Make sure these are the same embroidered flower patterns. Repeat for the other two sides.

5. Pin and sew one Blue 3" x 28" outer border strip in place. Repeat for opposite side. Press. Repeat for the other two sides using 33" border strips.

6. Layer backing, batting and top to form a sandwich. Baste the layers together. Quilt as desired. Trim the backing and batting to the edge of the quilt top.

7. Sew binding strips into one long piece. Press binding in half lengthwise. Using a ¼" seam allowance, sew binding to the quilt front. Turn to the back and hem by hand.

Blue Basket Quilt

A Lovely Blue Basket
see photo page 18

Blue Basket Quilt Assembly

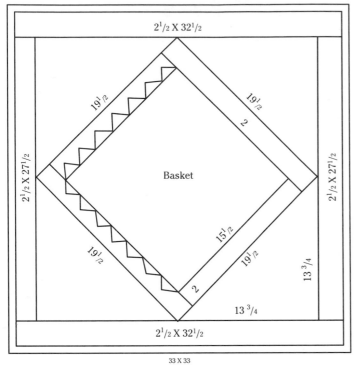

$2^1/2$ X $32^1/2$

$19^1/2$

$19^1/2$

2

$2^1/2$ X $27^1/2$

Basket

$2^1/2$ X $27^1/2$

$15^1/2$

$13^3/4$

$19^1/2$

$19^1/2$

2

$13^3/4$

$2^1/2$ X $32^1/2$

33 X 33

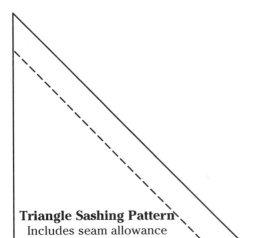

Triangle Sashing Pattern
Includes seam allowance

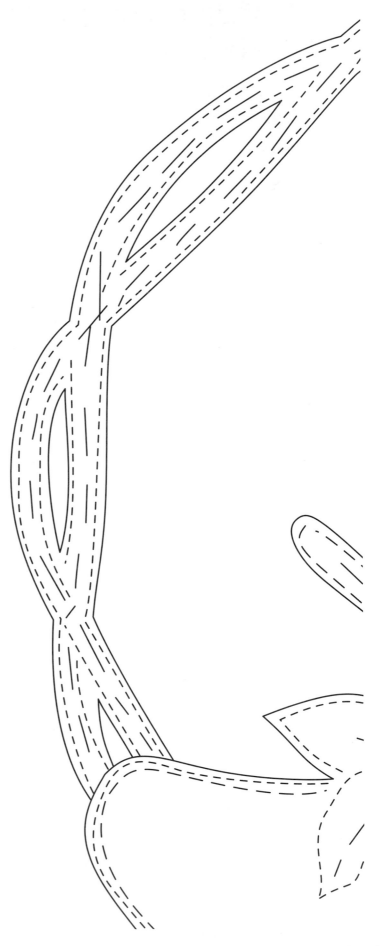

Blue Basket with Flowers

Pattern continues on pages 22-23.

A Lovely Blue Basket

see photo page 18

Pattern continued from pages 20-21.

Tied Tulips - Transfer 2

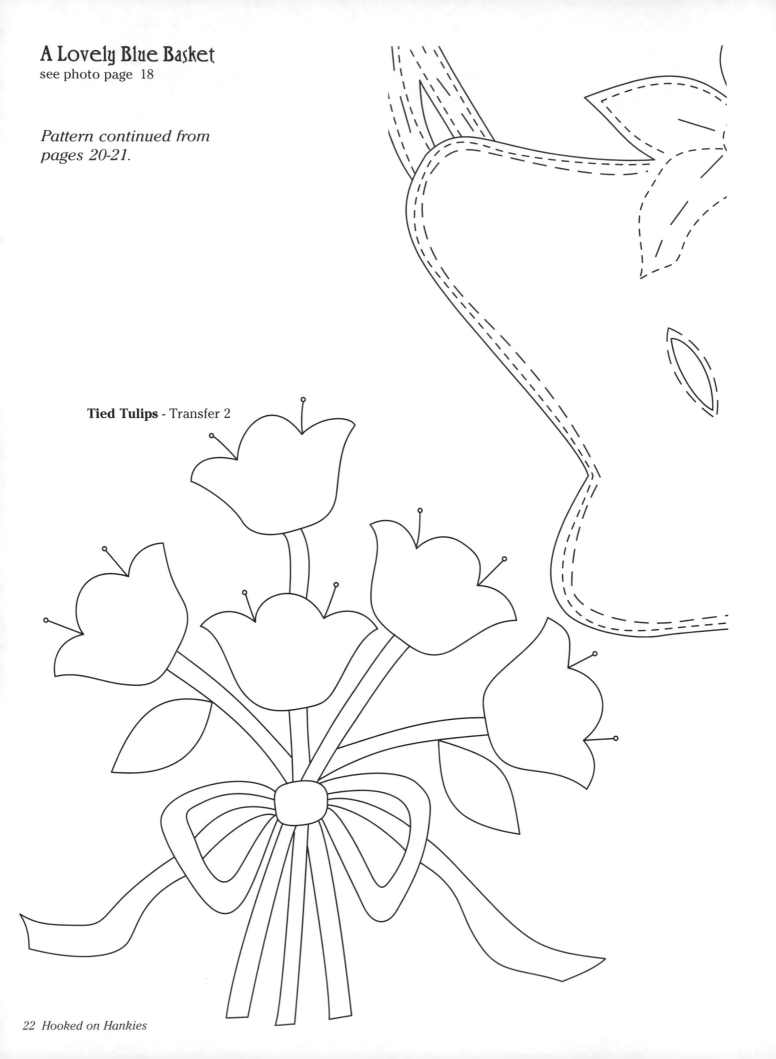

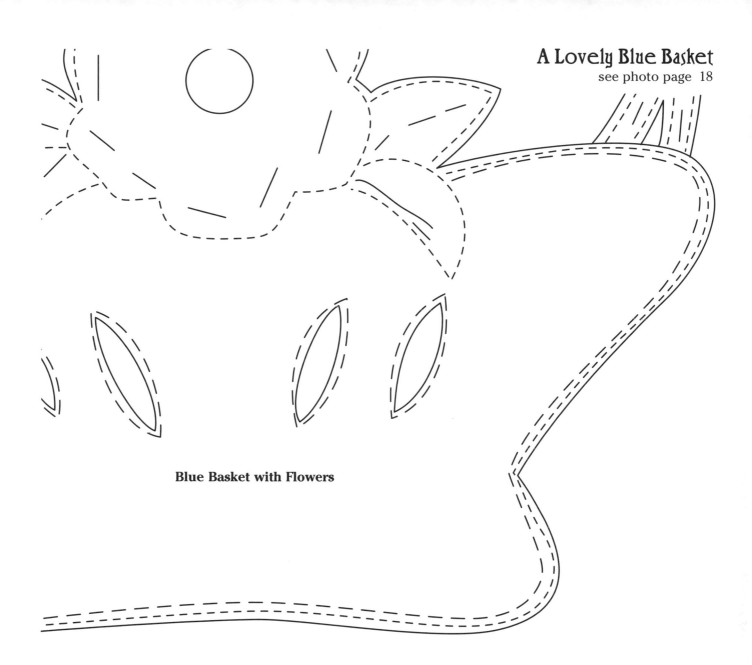

Blue Basket with Flowers

A Tisket, a tasket, a Lovely Blue Basket
I wrote a letter to my love
   but on the way I lost it!

A Tisket, a tasket, a Lovely Blue Basket
I filled the basket with flowers for my true love,
   but on the way I lost it!

A Lovely Blue Basket
see photo page 18

Tied Flowers - Transfer 2

FINISHED SIZE: 18½" x 60½"
FABRICS:
14 Handkerchiefs in coordinating colors
1½ yards Tan for embroidered rectangle
2 yards Red for borders, binding and backing
Batting
MATERIALS:
Embroidery floss to match Red fabric
Size 8 embroidery needle
Freezer paper

CUTTING: (See Cutting Diagram)
1 Tan 6½" x 48½" piece for center panel
1 Red 20" x 63" piece for backing
2 Red 1½" x 6½" strips for first border
2 Red 1½" x 50½" strip for first border
2 Red 4½" x 8½" strips for zigzag border
2 Red 4½" x 58½" strips for zigzag border
2 Red 1½" x 16½" strips for outer border
2 Red 1½" x 61" strips for outer border
Red 2½" strips sewn together to make 162" of binding

INSTRUCTIONS:

1. Follow the Basic How-Tos for backing the Tan rectangle and transferring embroidery designs. Embroider and press. Trim rectangle to 6½" x 48½".

2. Sew 2 Red 1½" x 6½" border strips to top and bottom of Tan rectangle. Press. Sew 2 Red 1½" x 50½" strips to each side of Tan rectangle. Press.

3. Cut handkerchief corners off using the triangle pattern. Save the center section of the handkerchiefs to use later in the project. Position the diagonal edge of hankie along the 8½" edge of Red rectangle. Match dots on template with ¼" intersection points. Pin.

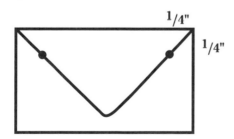

4. Sew down the hemmed edge of handkerchief with a Blind Hem stitch. Repeat for other rectangle. Sew rectangles to the top and bottom. Press.

5. Measure and mark 4½" from long end of Red zigzag border piece. Position the diagonal edge of the hanky, matching dots on the template along the ¼" and 4½" intersection. Pin hanky in place. Repeat at other end.

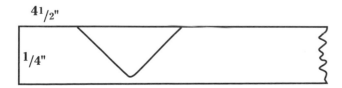

6. Place 5 handkerchief corners in-between making their corners touch or slightly overlap. Pin. Sew down the hemmed edges of handkerchiefs with a Blind Hem stitch. Sew hanky edge to the left 1" Red inner border. Press.

7. Along the outer edge of the Red 4½" border strip, lay a handkerchief corner between each one of the sewn ones. Adjust as necessary so that there is 1" of Red fabric showing between the two rows of handkerchiefs. Refer to the photo for placement. Press.

8. Repeat step 4 and 5 for the other Red strip, which is sewn onto the right side.

Hanky Center   **Hanky Center**

9. Diagonally fold one of the handkerchief centers (This was leftover from cutting off the corners). Crease. Add ¼" seam allowance beyond the fold and cut on this line. Lay it on the outside corner adjusting if necessary so that there is 1" of Red fabric showing between the hankies in the corner also. Pin. Sew using a Blind Hem stitch. Repeat for each corner. Note: my handkerchief leftovers weren't quite large enough so I sewed a narrow White strip to the long edge of the triangle and turned that under and appliqued it in place. Depending on the size of your hankies, you may have to sew 2 centers together to get them big enough.

10. Sew two Red 1½" x 16½" outer border strips to the top and bottom. Press. Repeat for the two Red side borders. Press.

11. Layer backing, batting and top to form a sandwich. Baste layers together. Quilt as desired. Trim the backing and batting to the edge of the quilt top.

12. Sew binding strips into one long piece. Press binding in half lengthwise. Use ¼" seam allowance and sew binding to the quilt front. Turn to back. Hem by hand.

Redwork Fruit Table Runner/Wall Hanging

see photo page 4

Grapes Pattern

Redwork Fruit Table Quilt Assembly

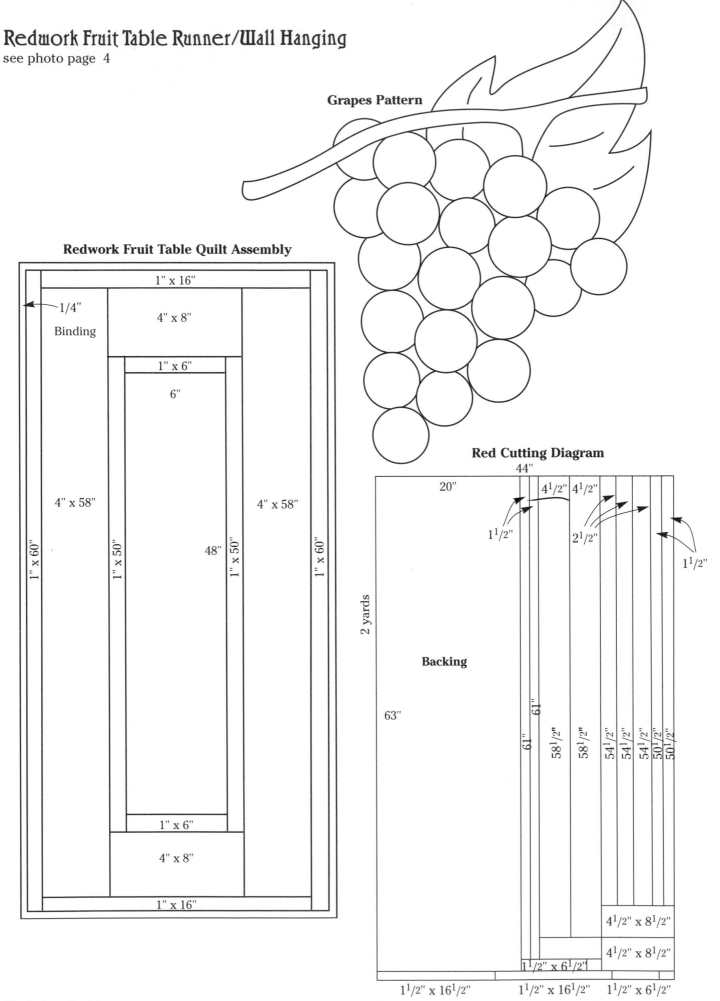

1" x 16"

← 1/4"

Binding

4" x 8"

1" x 6"

6"

4" x 58"   4" x 58"

1" x 60"   1" x 50"   48"   1" x 50"   1" x 60"

1" x 6"

4" x 8"

1" x 16"

Red Cutting Diagram

44"

20"

4¹/₂"   4¹/₂"

1¹/₂"

2¹/₂"

1¹/₂"

2 yards

Backing

63"

61"   61"

58¹/₂"

58¹/₂"

54¹/₂"   54¹/₂"

54¹/₂"   50¹/₂"   50¹/₂"

4¹/₂" x 8¹/₂"

4¹/₂" x 8¹/₂"

1¹/₂" x 6¹/₂"

1¹/₂" x 16¹/₂"   1¹/₂" x 16¹/₂"   1¹/₂" x 6¹/₂"

Peaches Pattern

Strawberry Pattern

Redwork Fruit Table Runner/Wall Hanging
see photo page 4

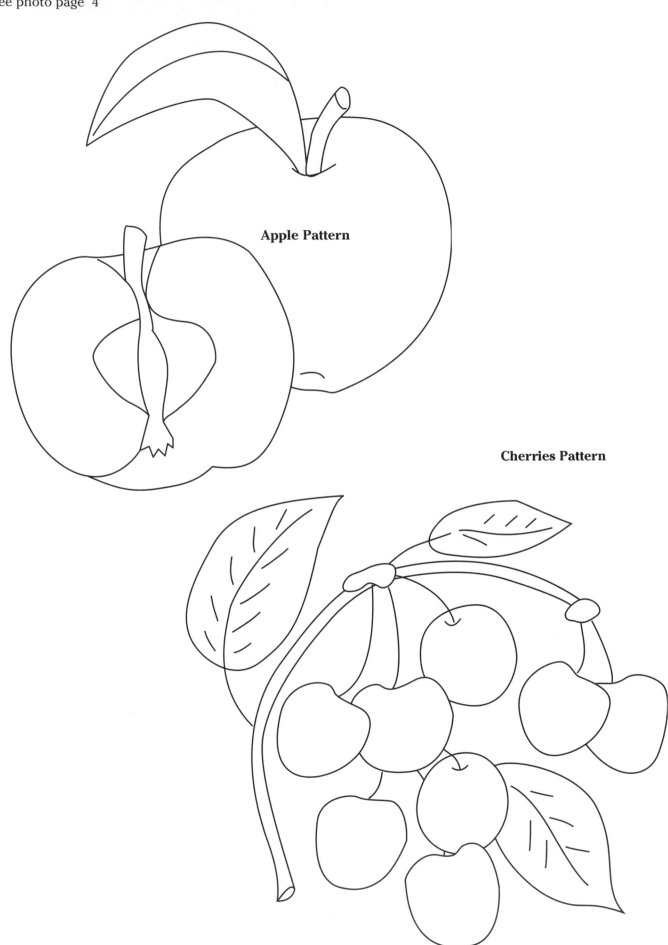

Apple Pattern

Cherries Pattern

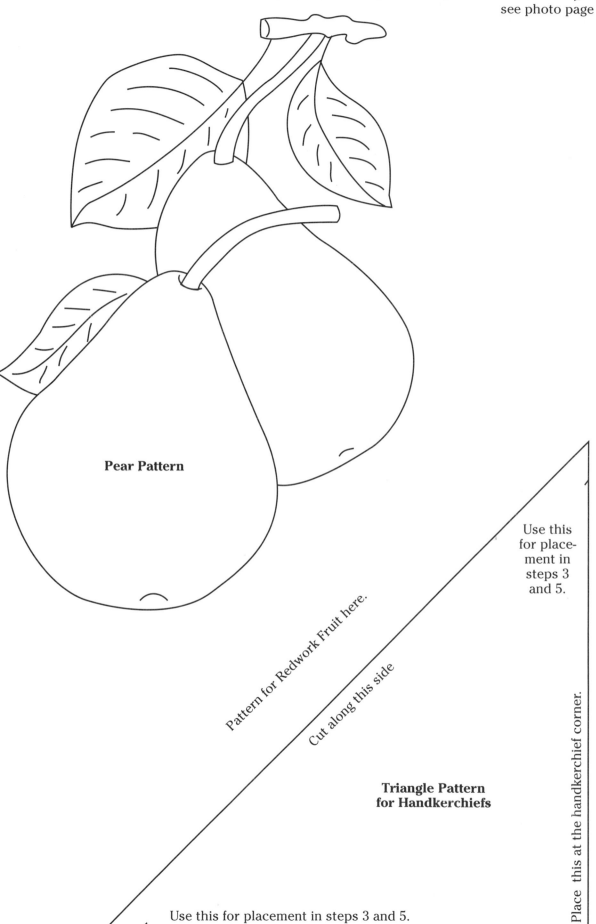

Pear Pattern

Pattern for Redwork Fruit here.

Cut along this side

Use this for placement in steps 3 and 5.

Triangle Pattern for Handkerchiefs

Place this at the handkerchief corner.

Use this for placement in steps 3 and 5.

Amy's Adventures

see photo page 5

designed by Janice Beals

FINISHED SIZE: 78" x 78"

FABRICS:
13 Handkerchiefs with beautiful edges for skirts
2½ yards White for blocks
2¼ yards Green for sashing, border and binding
⅓ yard Red for border
¼ yard Blue for border
2¼ yards Backing using 90" wide fabric
Batting

MATERIALS:
DMC embroidery floss (#407 Flesh, #301 Hair)
Embroidery floss in colors to match handkerchiefs
Embroidery needle size 8
Applique needle size 11 sharp
.01 Brown *Pigma* pen for inking details
Freezer paper

INSTRUCTIONS:

1. Follow the Basic How-Tos for backing each White square with freezer paper and transferring the embroidery designs.

Embroider and press. Do not embroider her eyes, eyebrows or mouth.

Press freezer paper on the back to keep the fabric from moving.

Use a Brown pen to ink her mouth, eyes, eyebrows, and details.

Remove the freezer paper when finished and heat set the block.

2. To applique handkerchief skirt:

a. Make a freezer paper pattern of the skirt and adapt the pattern to the handkerchief.

For example, the shoes may be covered up, or the tops may need to be extended to reach the hanky.

Since you are working on the bias, be careful not to stretch the hankies out of shape.

b. Cut out the skirt adding a ⅛" seam allowance. Pin in place and applique using the needle turn stitch.

Decorative edged handkerchiefs are often hemmed with a machine Satin stitch around a thin cord.

Use a Whipstitch to applique these types of edges. Press.

c. You may want to outline the skirts with a darker embroidery thread and a Backstitch for emphasis.

d. Trim squares to 12½" x 12½".

3. Sashing:

a. Sew Green 12½" sashing pieces to top left of each block.

b. Sew Green 12½" pieces to the bottom right of blocks 3, 8, 11, 12, 13. Press toward sashing.

c. Sew Green 16½" sashing pieces to top right side of block 3 and the bottom left side of block 11.

d. Sew sashing/block units to each other forming a row. Press.

e. Row 2 uses blocks 6, 9, 12. Sew Green 44½" sashing to the left side of Row 2.

CUTTING:
13 White 13½" x 13½" squares
2 White 21⅛" x 21⅛" squares for quilt side triangles
    then cut squares diagonally in half in each direction
2 White 12½" x 12½" squares for quilt corner triangles
    then cut squares in half diagonally
18 Green 2½" x 12½" strips for sashing
2 Green 2½" x 16½" strips for sashing
2 Green 2½" x 44½" strips for sashing
2 Green 2½" x 72½" strips for sashing (piece if necessary)
8 Green 2½" x 44" strips for first border
8 Red 1½" x 44" for second border
8 Blue 1" x 44" for third border
8 Green 4½" x 44" for 4th border
8 Green 2½" strips x 44" for the binding

Cut 21⅛" White squares   Cut 12½" White squares

f. Row 3 uses blocks 1, 4, 7, 10, 13. Sew Green 72½" sashing to the left side of Row 3.

g. Sew Green 72½" sashing to the right side of Row 3. Press.

h. Row 4 uses blocks 2, 5, 8. Sew Green 44½" sashing strip to the right side of Row 4. Press.

i. Sew a large White triangle to the top of sashing on blocks 11, 6, 2, and 3.

j. Sew a large White triangle to the bottom of sashing below blocks 11, 12, 8, and 3. Press.

k. Sew the rows together as shown in the diagram.

l. Sew small White triangle to the top of sashing above block 1.

m. Sew small White triangle to the bottom of sashing below block 13.

n. Sew small White triangle to the left side of block 11.

o. Sew small White triangle to the right side of block 3. Trim to size if necessary. Press.

4. Border:

a. Sew Green 2½" strips end to end to make 4 pieces 77" long.

b. Sew Red 1½" strips end to end to make 4 pieces 77" long.

c. Sew Blue 1" strips end to end to make 4 pieces 77" long.

d. Sew Green 4½" strips end to end to make 4 pieces 77" long.

e. Sew 4 border sections together in this order: Green 2½", Red 1½", Blue 1", Green 4½".

f. Sew borders to the quilt and miter the corners.

5. Layer backing, batting and top to form a sandwich. Baste layers together. Quilt as desired.

Trim the backing and batting to the edge of the quilt top.

6. Sew binding strips into a strip 8¾ yards (314") long. Press binding in half lengthwise.

Use ⅜" seam allowance and sew binding to the quilt front. Turn to back. Hem by hand.

Quilt Assembly Diagram

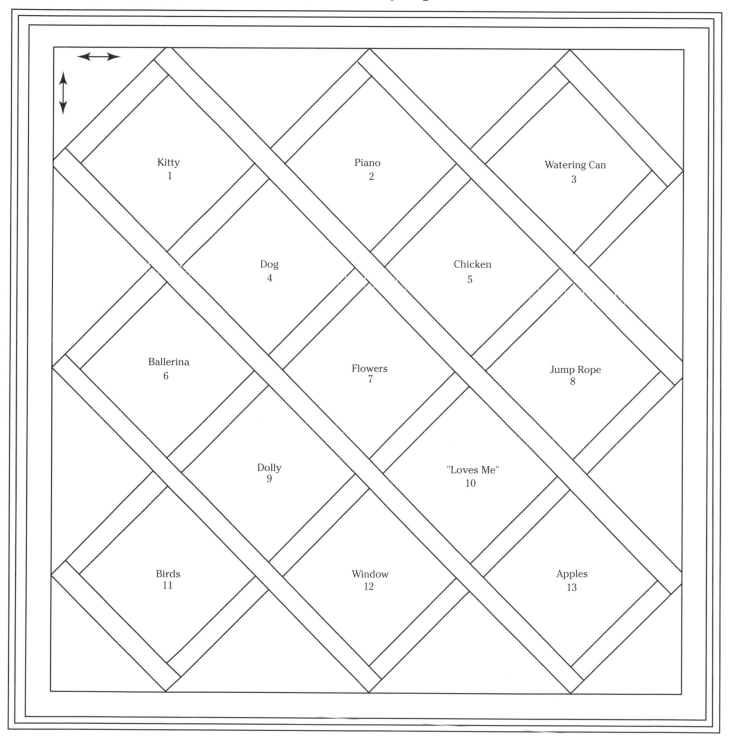

Kitty
1

Piano
2

Watering Can
3

Dog
4

Chicken
5

Ballerina
6

Flowers
7

Jump Rope
8

Dolly
9

"Loves Me"
10

Birds
11

Window
12

Apples
13

Amy's Adventures

see photo page 5

Enlarge
Amy's Adventures patterns on a
copy machine at 133 % for
actual size patterns.

HERE
KITTY KITTY

Kitty Pattern
1

LACE

Enlarge
Amy's Adventures patterns on a
copy machine at 133 % for
actual size patterns.

Piano Pattern
2

Amy's Adventures

see photo page 5

Enlarge
Amy's Adventures patterns on a
copy machine at 133 % for
actual size patterns.

Watering Can Pattern
3

Enlarge
Amy's Adventures patterns on a
copy machine at 133 % for
actual size patterns.

Dog Pattern
4

Amy's Adventures

see photo page 5

Enlarge
Amy's Adventures patterns on a
copy machine at 133 % for
actual size patterns.

Chicken Pattern
5

Enlarge
Amy's Adventures patterns on a
copy machine at 133 % for
actual size patterns.

Ballerina Pattern
6

Amy's Adventures

see photo page 5

Enlarge
Amy's Adventures patterns on a
copy machine at 133 % for
actual size patterns.

Flowers Pattern
7

Enlarge
Amy's Adventures patterns on a
copy machine at 133 % for
actual size patterns.

Jump Rope Pattern
8

Amy's Adventures
see photo page 5

Enlarge
Amy's Adventures patterns on a
copy machine at 133 % for
actual size patterns.

Dolly Pattern
9

Enlarge
Amy's Adventures patterns on a
copy machine at 133 % for
actual size patterns.

LOVES ME

LOVES ME NOT

"Loves Me" Pattern
10

Amy's Adventures
see photo page 5

Enlarge
Amy's Adventures patterns on a
copy machine at 133 % for
actual size patterns.

Birds Pattern
11

Enlarge
Amy's Adventures patterns on a
copy machine at 133 % for
actual size patterns.

Window Pattern
12

Amy's Adventures
see photo page 5

see photo page 5

Enlarge
Amy's Adventures patterns on a
copy machine at 133 % for
actual size patterns.

Apples Pattern
13

Enlarge
Amy's Adventures patterns on a
copy machine at 133 % for
actual size patterns.

May Basket

see photo page 6

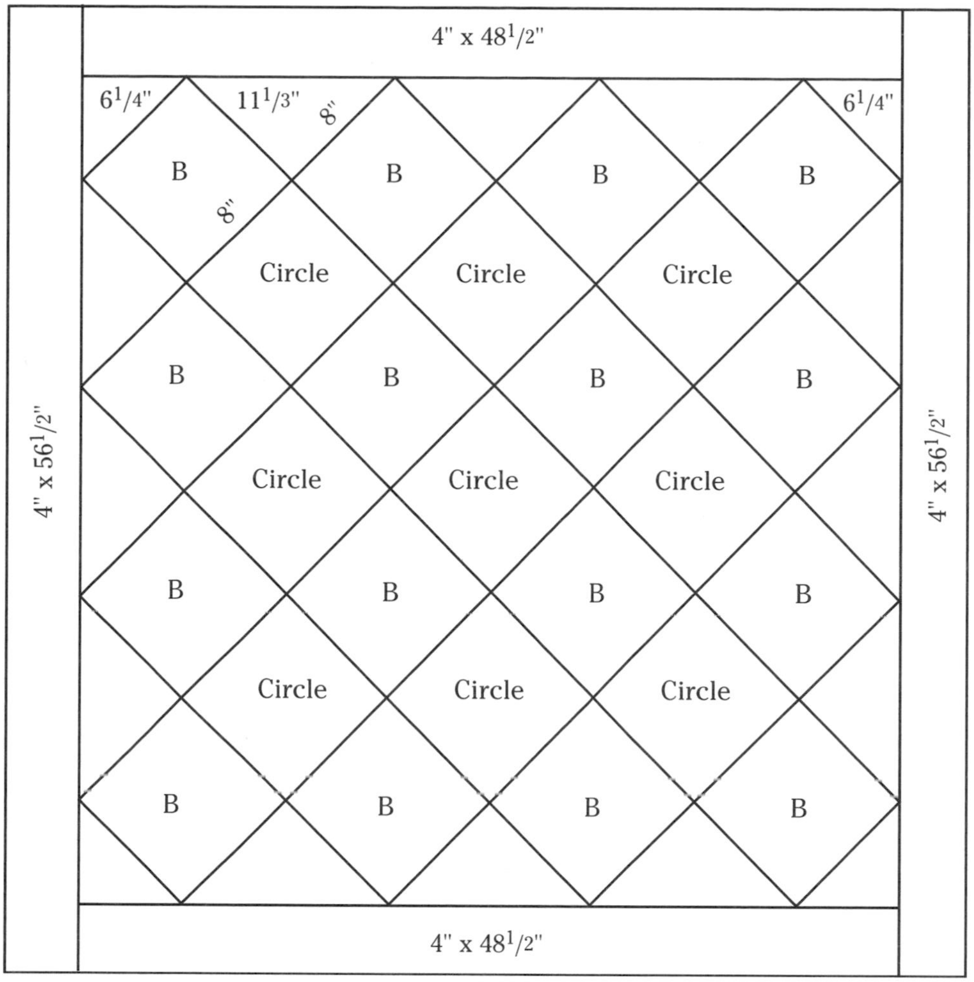

Quilt Assembly Diagram
57" x 57"
with binding

Diagram labels: 4" x 48½" (top and bottom borders), 4" x 56½" (side borders), 6¼", 11⅓", 8", 8", 6¼", with blocks labeled "B" and "Circle" in a diagonal grid.

FINISHED SIZE: 57" x 57"

FABRICS:

16 floral handkerchiefs

4⅛ yards White fabric for blocks, borders and binding

1⅔ yards White 60" wide fabric for backing

Batting

MATERIALS:

White embroidery floss to applique hankies and embroider basket handles

Embroidery floss to coordinate with handkerchief flowers

Embroidery needle size 8

Applique needle size 11 sharp

Freezer paper

CUTTING:

   25 White 9½" x 9½" blocks for applique and embroidery

   3 White 12½" x 12½" squares for triangles on the side of the quilt - then cut squares on both diagonals

   2 White 6¼" x 6¼" squares for triangles at the corners - then cut them in half diagonally

   2 White 4½" x 48½" strips for border

   2 White 4½" x 56½" strips for border

   6 White 2½" x 44" strips for binding

INSTRUCTIONS:

1. Cut handkerchiefs in half diagonally. Fold 16 White squares in half diagonally. Press fold.

   Center the cut edge of the handkerchief along the crease mark. Pin.

   Applique the hanky with a Blanket stitch using 2 strands of White floss.

2. Follow the Basic How-Tos for backing the 12 White squares with freezer paper.

   Transfer flower and basket handle embroidery designs.

Embroider the designs with the Stem stitch. Press.

   Trim squares to 8½" x 8½".

3. Follow the Basic How-Tos for backing the squares with the circular design.

   Embroider the motif using the Chain stitch. Press.

   Trim squares to 8½" x 8½".

4. Sew the row of blocks together adding solid triangles at the beginning of each row. Press.

   Trim triangles to size.

   Sew rows together. Press.

   Sew small triangles to each outer corner. Press.

   Trim triangles to size.

5. Sew the 48½" top and bottom border strips in place. Press.

   Sew the 56½" border strips to the sides.

6. Layer backing, batting and top to form a sandwich.

   Baste the layers together. Quilt as desired.

   Trim the batting and backing to the edge of the quilt top.

7. Sew binding strips into a 228" piece (6⅓ yards).

   Press binding in half lengthwise. Bind quilt.

Follow these steps to design the flowers to embroider based on your own handkerchiefs:

1. Select the dominant motif from the hanky that will fit within the arc of the basket.

2. Place tracing paper on top of the hanky and trace the design with pencil.

   Go over with an ink pen to clean up the lines and darken the motif.

3. Enlarge or reduce the drawing on a copy machine until you get the perfect size.

4. Follow the Basic How-Tos for transferring the design to the White square.

May Basket
see photo page 6

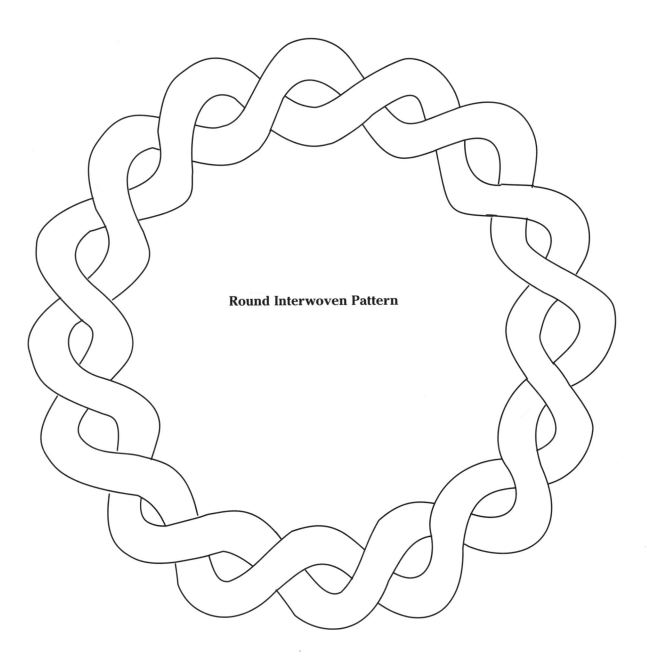

Round Interwoven Pattern

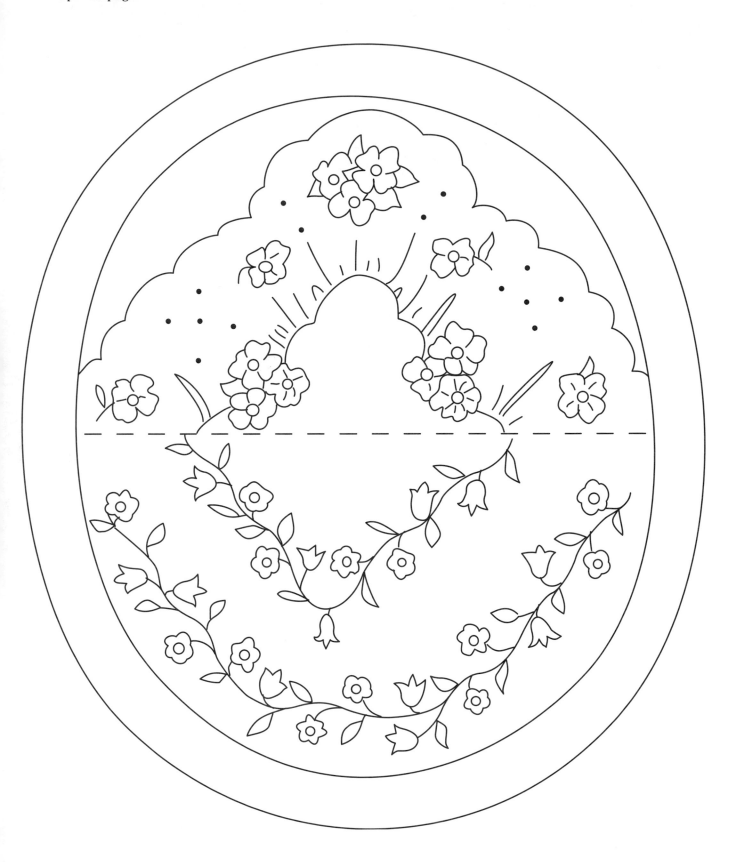

May Basket
see photo page 6

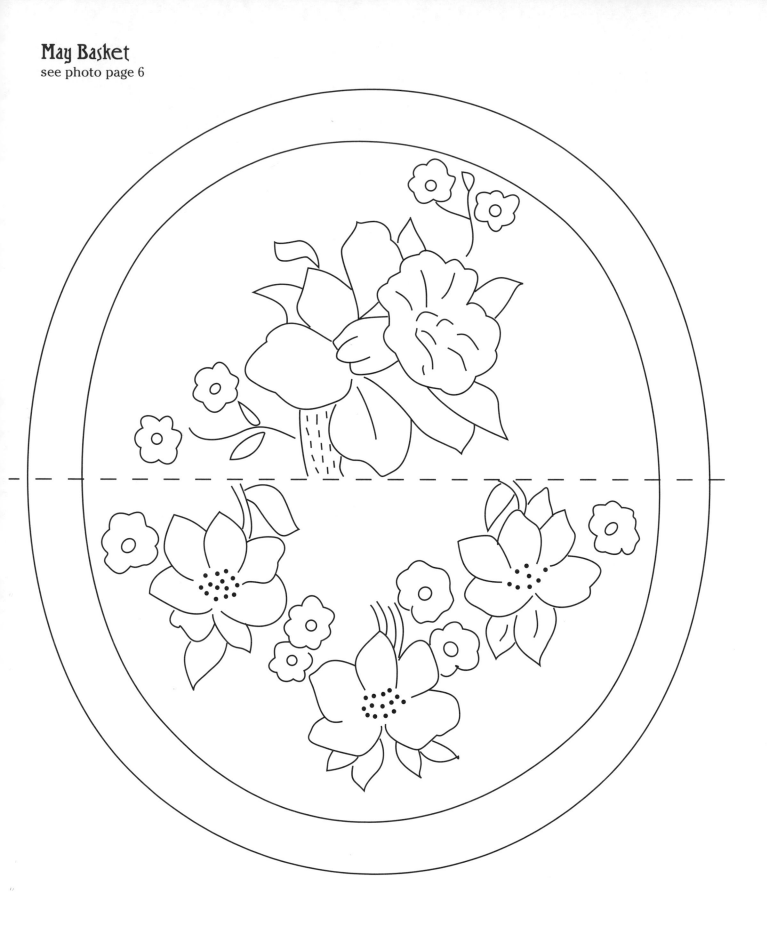

May Basket
see photo page 6

May Basket
see photo page 6

Those Adorable Waitresses

see photo page 7

FINISHED SIZE: 35" x 44"

FABRICS:

9 handkerchiefs (Don't forget to soak in Oxiclean.)
9 White cotton or linen shirts with a pocket
9 White shirts each with the same width button placket (Mine were 1½".)
⅓ yard Black cotton for binding
1⅜ yard White for backing
Batting

MATERIALS:

5 yards Black trim
DMC Black Pearl Cotton #5
Chenille needle size 22 for embroidery
Template plastic

INSTRUCTIONS:

1. Get pockets ready:

a. Measure 1½" from the right edge of the pocket and cut. Measure 1½" below pocket and cut.

b Cut top edge 12½" from bottom edge or at the place the arm curve cuts into the rectangle.

c. Cut left edge at 9½" from the right edge or at the place the buttons or placket get in the way.

d. If necessary, add rectangles to the left and top edge to make the pocket piece measure 9½" x 12½".

All but one of the pockets I used required adding these rectangles to make the block large enough. Press.

e. Using Black Pearl Cotton, outline the pocket with a Running stitch ⅟₁₆" away from the sewn pocket edge.

2. Button a shirt front together. Cut off placket close to the stitching. Cut off button layer slightly smaller.

Cut placket to 12½", centering the buttons so the placket above the top button equals the placket below the bottom button.

3. Position the placket on the pocket rectangle ¼" from the left edge. Pin.

Topstitch the placket in place sewing on top of the existing placket stitching.

Stitch again very close to the outer edge of the placket on both the left and right side. Repeat for all the pocket blocks.

4. Sew 3 pocket rectangles together to make a row. Make 3 rows and sew them together to make the nine-pocket quilt top.

5. Border:

a. Sew 9 rectangles in a row on the 4½" side for the top border. Repeat for the bottom.

b. Sew 12 together for one side. Repeat for the other side. Press.

c. Make zigzag pattern for small pocket border out of template plastic.

Position the template over the rectangles and lightly trace the zigzag design.

d. Measure 1¼" from the edge of the border and light-

Pocket Placement

```
        9 1/2"
   ┌─────────────────┐
   │          1 1/2" │
   │ 12        ┌───┐ │
   │ 1/2" │    │  ↓│ │
   │      │    │   │ │
   │      │    │   │ │
   │      │    └───┘ │
   │         1 1/2"  │
   └─────────────────┘
```

Tʜe pockets and plackets on this quilt come from real shirts. To give the quilt a rich texture, I chose shirts with different kinds of pockets and fabric weaves. Thanks to Joan Hahn for this great idea.

CUTTING:

4 Black 2½" x 44" binding strips
Using fabric leftover from all the shirts:
42 rectangles 3½" x 4½" for the border
4 squares 4½" x 4½" for the corners

ly draw a straight line across the entire pocket border.

e. Using Black Pearl Cotton, do a Running stitch on top of the marked lines and about ⅟₁₆" from each pocket side seam.

Refer to drawing. Stitch on all four borders.

f. Sew a 4½" square to each end of both side borders.

Mark each square with the corner design and stitch with Black Pearl Cotton.

6. Pin and sew the top and bottom borders onto the quilt top. Press. Repeat for the left and right borders. Press.

7. Topstitch the Black trim in place covering the border seams.

8. Layer backing, batting and top to form a sandwich. Baste layers together. Quilt as desired.

Trim the backing and batting to the edge of the quilt top.

9. Sew binding strips into one long piece. Press binding in half lengthwise.

Use ⅜" seam allowance and sew binding to the quilt front. Turn to back. Hem by hand.

Those Adorable Waitresses Quilt Assembly

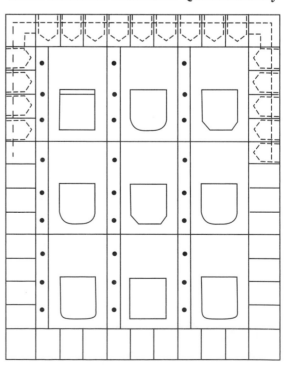

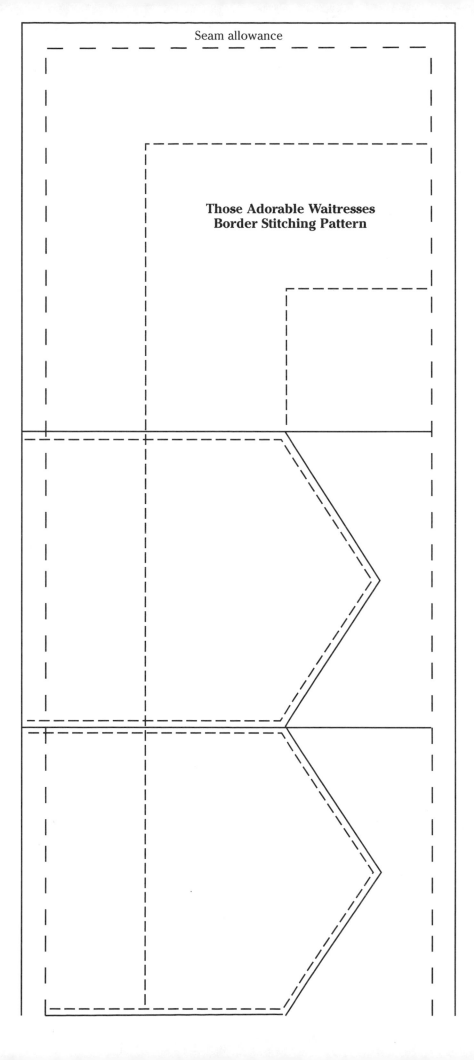

Seam allowance

**Those Adorable Waitresses
Border Stitching Pattern**

Wonderful Hanky Stories

My aunt tatted the edging around a white handkerchief for me when I got married. She was new at tatting and it took her a long time. She said that every time she checked the length, she only needed two more inches. She tatted that "two more inches" about six times.

At school, as part of hygiene class, the teacher inspected our hands and fingernails. If they passed her critical eye, she put a little drop of Lily of the Valley or Lavender fragrance on each girl's hanky.

One spring many years ago, Laurene and I were on a trip to the big quilt show in Paducah where she bought an antique handkerchief with lovely handmade edging and gave it to me. I've carried it with me ever since.

Mother didn't consider my sister and I completely dressed unless we had a handkerchief pinned at the waist of our dress. We didn't know what she expected us to do with them, but we couldn't leave the house without them.

Fran Techlow remembers: "Sometimes I was allowed to take the bus to visit my aunt who lived about 10 miles away. On those exciting occasions I was given Church money and spending money amounting to about 25 cents. This was always tied in the corner of my handkerchief, which was tied to my belt. I never lost a penny."

Tooth Fairy Pillow

FABRICS:
One 9½" handkerchief with lace edging
¼ yard White muslin

MATERIALS:
DMC floss to match lace edging
Fiberfill stuffing

CUTTING:
White Muslin:
    One 8½" square for the embroidered pillow top
    One 7½" square for the pillow back
    Two rectangles 2" x 2½" for pocket

INSTRUCTIONS:
1. Follow the Basic How-Tos for backing 8½" square and 1 White rectangle with freezer paper and transferring the embroidery design.
    Embroider and press. Trim the embroidered square to 7½".
2. With right sides together, sew the rectangles around the edge, leaving a hole for turning.
    Turn right side out. Whipstitch the pocket in place as shown in the photo.
3. With right sides together, sew the pillow top to the back, leaving a hole for turning.
    Turn right side out. Stuff with fiberfill. Whipstitch the opening closed.
4. Center the pillow on the handkerchief. Whipstitch the pillow to the handkerchief.

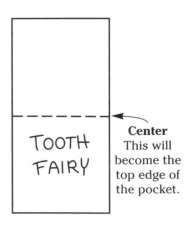

TOOTH FAIRY

Center
This will become the top edge of the pocket.

Baby Crib Bumper Pads & Tooth Fairy Pillow

see photo page 8

Flannel Quilt

see photo page 8

BABY CRIB BUMPER PADS
FABRICS:
1⅓ yard Handkerchief print fabric
MATERIALS:
Ready-made Blue denim bumper pads
INSTRUCTIONS:
1. Cut out 4 Handkerchief sections to fit across each long bumper pad. Cut 2 handkerchief sections to fit across each short end bumper pad.
   For each section, turn under the outside edge ¼" and hem by machine.
2. Center the handkerchief on each bumper pad. Pin in place.
   Sew it on by hand using a Whipstitch.
   Repeat for all bumper sections.

FINISHED SIZE: 36" x 36"
FABRICS:
1 yard printed handkerchief fabric
1⅓ yard Flannel for backing and binding
CUTTING:
36" square Flannel
36" square Handkerchief print.
4 strips 2⅜" x 44" Flannel for binding
INSTRUCTIONS:
1. Lay both fabrics wrong sides together. Pin.
2. Sew the binding strips to make 146".
   Press binding in half lengthwise.
   Sew to front using ⅜" seam allowance.
   Turn to back. Hem by hand.

TOOTH
FAIRY

Totebag

see photo page 8

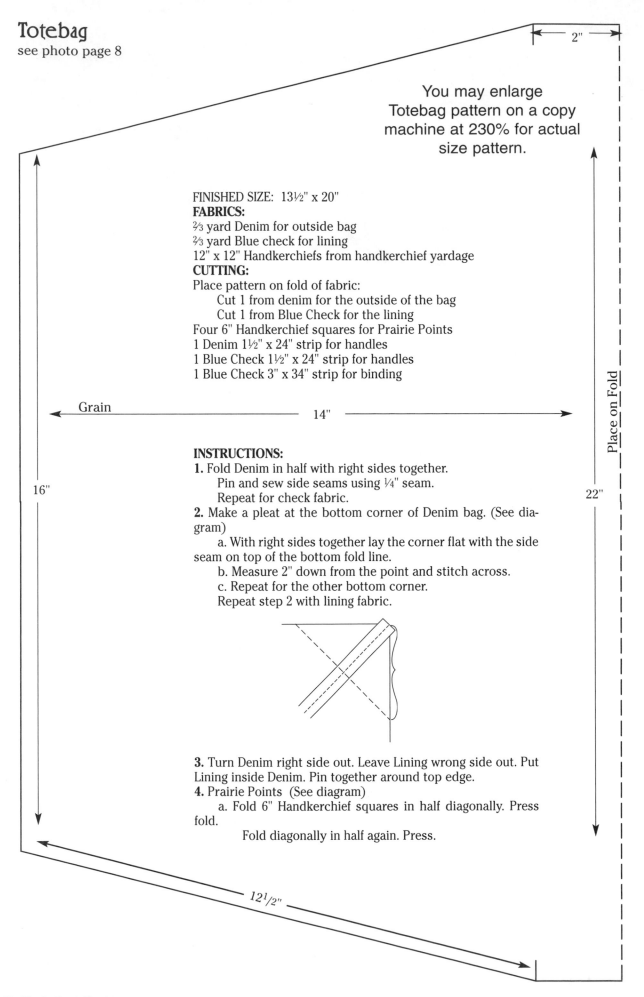

2"

You may enlarge
Totebag pattern on a copy
machine at 230% for actual
size pattern.

FINISHED SIZE: 13½" x 20"
FABRICS:
⅔ yard Denim for outside bag
⅔ yard Blue check for lining
12" x 12" Handkerchiefs from handkerchief yardage
CUTTING:
Place pattern on fold of fabric:
    Cut 1 from denim for the outside of the bag
    Cut 1 from Blue Check for the lining
Four 6" Handkerchief squares for Prairie Points
1 Denim 1½" x 24" strip for handles
1 Blue Check 1½" x 24" strip for handles
1 Blue Check 3" x 34" strip for binding

Grain

14"

Place on Fold

INSTRUCTIONS:
1. Fold Denim in half with right sides together.
    Pin and sew side seams using ¼" seam.
    Repeat for check fabric.
2. Make a pleat at the bottom corner of Denim bag. (See diagram)
    a. With right sides together lay the corner flat with the side seam on top of the bottom fold line.
    b. Measure 2" down from the point and stitch across.
    c. Repeat for the other bottom corner.
    Repeat step 2 with lining fabric.

16"

22"

3. Turn Denim right side out. Leave Lining wrong side out. Put Lining inside Denim. Pin together around top edge.
4. Prairie Points (See diagram)
    a. Fold 6" Handkerchief squares in half diagonally. Press fold.
        Fold diagonally in half again. Press.

12½"

Making Prairie Points

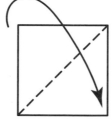

1. Fold the 6" hand-kerchief squares in half diagonally. Press folds.
2. Fold the squares in half again. Press.

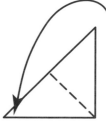

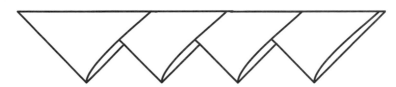

3. Align the prairie points side by side. Tuck one end of the point inside the open edge of the next point.

b. Place the prairie points side by side around the top edge of the bag with raw edges together.

Tuck one end of each triangle about halfway inside the open edge of the next triangle.

c. Stitch to bag.

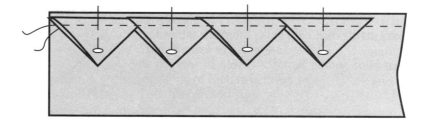

Sew the prairie points to the bag.

5. Press binding strip in half lengthwise.

Using ⅜" seam allowance, sew binding around the top of bag, hiding the Prairie Point seam.

Turn binding to the inside and hem by hand.

6. Place Lining and Denim handle strips right sides together.

Sew together on both long seams using ¼" seam allowance. Turn right side out. Press flat.

Cut in half, making two 1" x 12" pieces. Turn raw edges in ¼" and sew across both ends of each handle.

Topstitch close to both outside edges.

7. Pin handles to the inside of the bag. Lift hankies out of the way so stitching won't show.

Machine stitch them to the bag about 1½" below the top edge.

Baby Bonnets

see photo page 9

FINISHED SIZE: Newborn baby
FABRICS:
10" x 12" handkerchief with lace trim
MATERIALS:
1⅓ yard White satin ribbon ⅝" wide for ties
⅔ yard White sheer ribbon ¼" wide for gathering at back of
   baby's head
CUTTING:
Cut ⅝" ribbon into two 24" pieces.
INSTRUCTIONS:
1. Fold handkerchief in half. Press.
2. Sew a Running stitch across the hankie ½" above fold.
3. Fold the top layer of handkerchief back approximately 2" including lace. Stitch the folded section down along the lace at the sides.

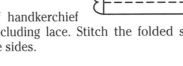

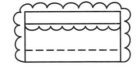

4. For each piece of ⅝" ribbon:
   Fold two 1" loops at one end.
   Whipstitch with matching thread around the base of the loops and pull tight.

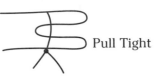
Pull Tight

5. Sew ribbon onto the front corner of the baby bonnet.
   Repeat for the other side.
   Scrunch loops so they look irregular and flower-shaped.
6. Run narrow ribbon through the channel made in step 2.
   Pull ribbon to gather bonnet to fit baby's head and tie in the back.
NOTE: To convert the bonnet to a bridal hanky, remove the stitching in step 2.

Christening Dress

see photo page 9

designed by Patty Harvey

FINISHED SIZE: Newborn
FABRICS:
Assorted White handkerchiefs with special edgings
   and embroidery
5 yards White batiste (refer to your pattern)
MATERIALS:
Baby dress pattern featuring a round yoke with
   back opening, puffed sleeves, and a slip.
   Choose a long dress style if possible.
1½ yards gathered ⅝" lace for neck and bottom of
   yoke
1½ yards straight ⅝" lace for sleeves
½ yard narrow elastic for sleeves
1 pkg bias tape for channel for elastic
Buttons or snaps for back closure
INSTRUCTIONS:
Use a ⅝" seam allowance for sewing this garment together.
Follow instructions included with your pattern noting the following adaptations:
1. Cut out dress pieces making sure the length of the skirt from the yoke is 24" or longer. Extend the length if necessary.
   Sew the skirt pieces together at the sides using a French seam.
2. Lay the skirt flat and shape the back into a gentle curve.
3. Plan how many handkerchiefs you need before you cut any.
   a. The handkerchiefs are smallest at the yoke and get larger as they come down the center back.
      Adjust the size and number of the squares as needed for the length and fullness of the skirt pattern.
   b. Cut squares out of one corner of the handkerchief.
      The top square on our dress is cut 2½", next square 3¼", next 4¼" next 4½".
      Adjust the size of the squares and the number of the squares you need until you reach the center front.
      The center front square is cut 7¼".

Left Back Section of Skirt | Right Back Section of Skirt

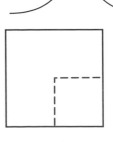
Hanky corner removed.

c. Fold the two cut sides of each hanky under ¼". Press.

4. Measure ⅝" from the top edge of the right back skirt opening.

Position smallest hanky so the 2 folded sides extend onto the dress and the 2 finished sides extend beyond it.

Place the wrong side of hanky to the right side of skirt. Pin.

Topstitch the hanky in place on the 2 sides that overlap the skirt fabric.

Continue using graduated sizes going down the back. Repeat for the left back opening.

Continue across the front of the skirt also.

5. Trim the dress fabric under the handkerchiefs leaving a ¼" seam allowance.

Whipstitch or machine zigzag the raw edges of the dress and handkerchief together.

6. Handkerchief corners also come down the center front of the dress.

To form the top square, cut 2 triangle corners off a handkerchief using the triangle pattern.

Sew them together to make a 4" square.

7. The other squares on the dress front are cut the same as in step 3 in the following sizes: 4¾", 5¼", and 6¼".

Turn under the 2 cut raw edges of the handkerchiefs ¼". Press.

Lay the handkerchiefs from the bottom up, overlapping the previous one. (See photo.)

Position the two-triangle square last ending ⅝" below the top edge. Topstitch the hankies in place.

Trim the fabric underneath so there is only one layer. Whipstitch or zigzag the raw edges as in step 5.

8. Lay yoke pieces flat and position a handkerchief on each section as desired.

Trim handkerchief to match the yoke pieces. Repeat for the sleeve pieces.

9. Finish assembling the dress according to your pattern instructions using French seams wherever possible.

Remember to insert gathered lace at the neck and at the bottom of the yoke.

Also apply ungathered lace to the bottom edge of sleeve.

10. Construct the slip following your pattern instructions.

Attach handkerchiefs the same way as the dress around just the bottom of the slip.

Adjust the size of the squares to fit the width of the slip.

Our handkerchief corners were cut at 5" (finished at 4¾") and ours took 10.

11. For a lovely finishing touch, embroider the baby's name and birth date along the bottom of the dress.

Christening Dress
see photo page 9

designed by Patty Harvey

Right Back Skirt

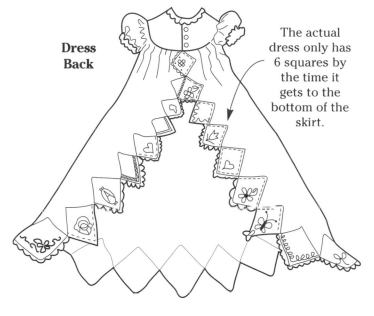

Dress Back

The actual dress only has 6 squares by the time it gets to the bottom of the skirt.

Yoke

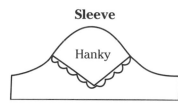

Neck Opening — Hanky

Sleeve

Hanky

Slip

4"

4"

Christening Dress Pattern
Cut 2

4" Square at Top of hankies going down the center front
Use this in Step 6.

Bluework Kids

see photo page 10

FINISHED SIZE: 31" x 31"

FABRICS:
4 Handkerchiefs as close to the same size as possible
2¼ yards Blue polka dot for front, back and binding
¼ yard White for embroidered squares

MATERIALS:
4 yards Blue satin ribbon ¼" wide
Embroidery needle size 8
Embroidery floss to match Blue fabric
Batting
Freezer paper

CUTTING:
1 Blue 32" x 32" square for quilt top
4 White 8" x 9" rectangles for embroidery
1 Blue 36" x 36" square for backing
3 Blue 2⅜" x 44" for 126" of binding

INSTRUCTIONS:
1. Follow the Basic How-Tos for backing the White rectangles and transferring the embroidery designs.
   Embroider using 2 strands of floss. Press. Trim rectangles to 7" x 8".
2. Center rectangles on handkerchiefs.
   Sew onto hanky ⅛" from the edge using a Running stitch.
   Sew on ¼" wide Blue ribbon over the stitching and raw edge using a tiny Tacking stitch. Press.
3. Position hankies on 32" quilt top. Refer to photo for placement. Pin.
   Applique hankies using a Tacking stitch. Press.
4. Layer backing, batting and top to form a sandwich.
   Baste layers together. Quilt as desired.
   Trim batting and backing to the edge of quilt top.
5. Sew binding strips into a 126" strip.
   Press binding in half lengthwise.
   Use ⅜" or ¼" seam allowance and sew binding to the quilt front.
   Turn to back. Hem by hand.

Heart Pillow

see photo page 11

designed by Sandra Streech

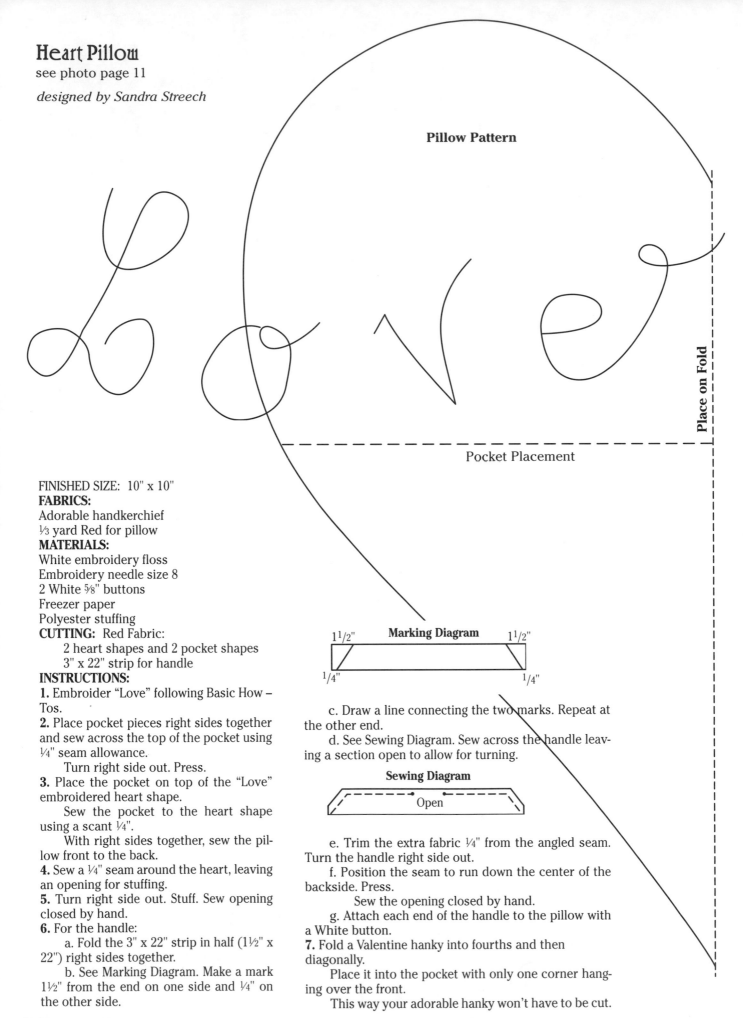

Pillow Pattern

Place on Fold

Pocket Placement

Marking Diagram

1¹/₂"   1¹/₂"

¹/₄"   ¹/₄"

Sewing Diagram

Open

FINISHED SIZE: 10" x 10"
FABRICS:
Adorable handkerchief
¹/₃ yard Red for pillow
MATERIALS:
White embroidery floss
Embroidery needle size 8
2 White ⁵/₈" buttons
Freezer paper
Polyester stuffing
CUTTING: Red Fabric:
    2 heart shapes and 2 pocket shapes
    3" x 22" strip for handle
INSTRUCTIONS:
1. Embroider "Love" following Basic How – Tos.
2. Place pocket pieces right sides together and sew across the top of the pocket using ¹/₄" seam allowance.
    Turn right side out. Press.
3. Place the pocket on top of the "Love" embroidered heart shape.
    Sew the pocket to the heart shape using a scant ¹/₄".
    With right sides together, sew the pillow front to the back.
4. Sew a ¹/₄" seam around the heart, leaving an opening for stuffing.
5. Turn right side out. Stuff. Sew opening closed by hand.
6. For the handle:
    a. Fold the 3" x 22" strip in half (1¹/₂" x 22") right sides together.
    b. See Pillow Diagram. Make a mark 1¹/₂" from the end on one side and ¹/₄" on the other side.

c. Draw a line connecting the two marks. Repeat at the other end.
    d. See Sewing Diagram. Sew across the handle leaving a section open to allow for turning.

e. Trim the extra fabric ¹/₄" from the angled seam. Turn the handle right side out.
    f. Position the seam to run down the center of the backside. Press.
        Sew the opening closed by hand.
    g. Attach each end of the handle to the pillow with a White button.
7. Fold a Valentine hanky into fourths and then diagonally.
    Place it into the pocket with only one corner hanging over the front.
    This way your adorable hanky won't have to be cut.

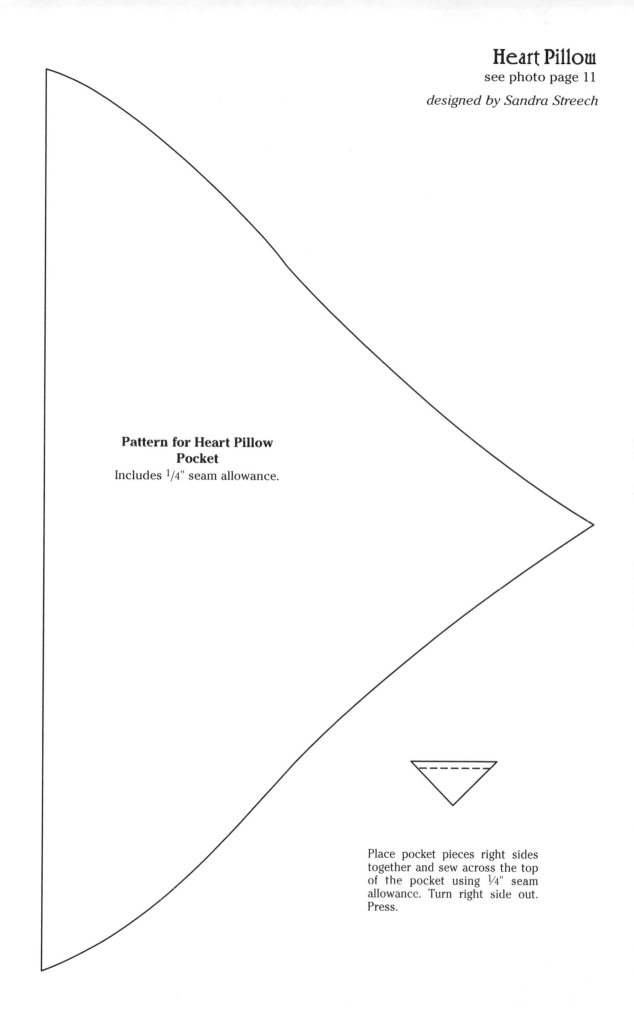

Heart Pillow
see photo page 11

designed by Sandra Streech

**Pattern for Heart Pillow
Pocket**
Includes 1/4" seam allowance.

Place pocket pieces right sides together and sew across the top of the pocket using 1/4" seam allowance. Turn right side out. Press.

Handkerchief Wreath & Curtain
see photo page 11

WREATH
FINISHED SIZE: 20" x 20"
FABRICS:
48 handkerchiefs
MATERIALS:
14" flat wire wreath form
16 yards grosgrain ribbon ⅜" wide
INSTRUCTIONS:
1. Open up a handkerchief and roll it on the diagonal to make it long and narrow.

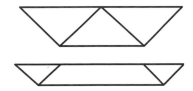

2. Visually divide the wreath into 8 sections. Use 6 handkerchiefs to cover each section.

Wrap handkerchief around the wreath form and tie a half knot on top. Repeat until form is covered.
3. Cut ribbon into twenty-four 24" lengths.

Place one piece around the wreath form between every other handkerchief and tie it into a bow.
4. To make the wreath look full and fluffy, go back and spread open each handkerchief corner.
5. If the wreath flattens and looks limp after a while, turn it upside down and shake it a couple of times.

If the humidity is high, press the hankies with starch or fabric sizing to keep them crisp.

CURTAIN
FINISHED SIZE: 48" x 84"
FABRICS:
28 Handkerchiefs 12" square or handkerchief yardage
MATERIALS:
8 yards Blue and White checked wire edged ribbon 1½" wide
INSTRUCTIONS:
1. Place 2 handkerchiefs right side up. Overlap their hemmed edges about ½". Pin.

Sew through both hankies next to both sides of the overlapped area making a mock French seam.

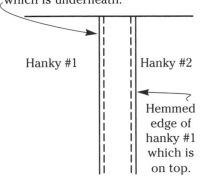

Hemmed edge of hanky #2 which is underneath.

Hanky #1   Hanky #2

Hemmed edge of hanky #1 which is on top.

2. Sew 4 handkerchiefs together to make a row. Then sew 7 rows together to make the curtain.
3. Cut the ribbon into 8 pieces each 1 yard long. Divide ribbon at halfway point.

Pin the ribbon to the top corner of each handkerchief and at the beginning and ending corners. Sew.
4. Tie ribbon in bows over a curtain rod.

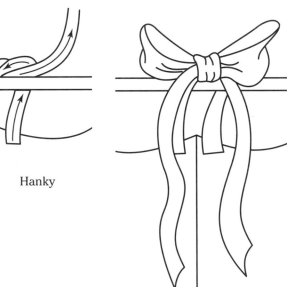

Sew ribbon to hanky and tie in an overhand knot.

Tie in a bow.

Hanky   Hanky

FINISHED SIZE: 18½" x 29"

MATERIALS:

Tea towel
Two coordinated handkerchiefs
Floss to match Red in towel
Size 8 embroidery needle
Freezer paper
.01 Red *Pigma* pen

INSTRUCTIONS:

1. Embroider the bird on the tea towel following Basic How-Tos.
  Trace the design on the right side of fabric with *Pigma* pen.
  Embroider the design using 2 strands of floss.
  Use care when pulling the stitches snug in coarsely woven fabric. Press.

2. Cut handkerchiefs in half.
  Place 3 corners across one end of towel with handkerchief's wrong side on towel's wrong side.
  Overlap handkerchiefs to fit.
  Stitch handkerchiefs to towel right above the towel hemline.

3. Press handkerchiefs down.
  Trim the handkerchief seam allowance in half.
  Top stitch the layers together at bottom edge by sewing over the towel's bottom hem stitching.
  Repeat steps 2 and 3 for the other end.

4. Embroider the little running vine to camouflage the stitched edge.

**Tea Towel
Vine Pattern**

Every Sunday, money for church was always tied into the corner of a hanky and then tied around my waist to my dress sash.

Lampshade and Pillows
see photo page 12

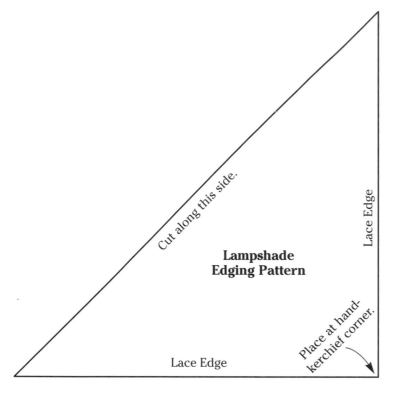

Lampshade Edging Pattern

Cut along this side.

Lace Edge

Lace Edge

Lace Edge

Place at handkerchief corner.

Lace Edge

LAMPSHADE
FINISHED SIZE: Any lamp with shade will work
FABRIC: Handkerchiefs with handmade lace edgings
   3 hanky corners for every 5" of bottom circumference on the shade
MATERIALS:
Lamp base with shade
Trim to go around the top and bottom of the shade
Hot glue gun
INSTRUCTIONS:
1. Cut off the corners of the handkerchiefs using the triangle pattern.
2. Run a short bead of glue at the bottom edge of the shade along the side.
   Gather the edge of the hanky slightly as you press it into the glue.
   To placed hankies evenly, think of a clock. Place a hanky at 12, 3, 6, and 9.
   Fill the gaps with more hanky corners, overlapping the ends about ¼".
3. Hot glue trim to cover the raw edge of the handkerchiefs.
   Glue additional piece of trim to the top edge if desired.

ENVELOPE PILLOW
Hankie Doodle Design by Nancy Eshelman
FINISHED SIZE: LAVENDER & GREEN 11" x 15"
PINK 10½" x 13½
FABRICS:
Lace edge hankie with corner motif:
    10" for Lavender and Green pillow
    9" for Pink pillow
⅓ yard print for pillow front and back
⅓ yard Lavender or Pink print for envelope triangle
    and bias binding

ENVELOPE PILLOW
MATERIALS:
1 yard Cording ½" wide
Buttons
Embroidery floss
Pillow stuffing
CUTTING:
2 print rectangles for front and back:
    11½" x 15½" for Lavender and Green pillow
    11" x 14" for Pink pillow
1 Lavender or Pink print square 10½",
    cut across the diagonal

INSTRUCTIONS:
1. Lavender or Pink triangle:
   With right sides together, sew the the 2 short sides, leaving the long side open. Turn right side out and press.
   Fold the handkerchief on the diagonal as shown in the photo. Position the hanky on the Lavender triangle.
   Topstitch the lace edging to hold the hanky in place.
   Topstitch the hankie triangle to the front of the pillow along the long edge.
2. Bias cording:
   Cut bias strips of Lavender and sew them together to cover the cording.
   Stitch cording to the right side of the back of the pillow on 3 sides. (See photo.)
3. Pillow construction:
   With right sides together, cording inside, sew the back to the front leaving a 5" opening for turning.
   Turn the pillow right side out. Stuff. Sew the opening closed.
4. Embellishments: Using floss, sew buttons in place as desired.

NAVY BLUE PILLOW

Hankie Doodle Design by Nancy Eshelman

FINISHED SIZE: 15" x 15"

FABRICS:
12" printed hanky
½ yard print for back and cording
⅛ yard Check for border

MATERIALS:
1¾ yard Cording ½" wide
Buttons, Embroidery floss, Pillow stuffing

INSTRUCTIONS:

1. Top:

Sew the top and bottom borders to the hanky. Press. Sew the side borders to the hanky. Press.

Sew the buttons in the corners as desired.

2. Bias cording:

Stitch cording to the right side of the back of the pillow.

3. Pillow construction:

With right sides together, cording inside, sew the back to the front leaving a 5" opening for turning.

Turn the pillow right side out. Stuff. Sew the opening closed.

NAVY BLUE PILLOW

CUTTING:
Border rectangles: Cut 2 of each
2" x 12½" for top and bottom
2" x 15½" for side borders
Back: 15½" x 15½"
Cording: 2" wide bias strips sewn together to cover cording

see photo page 12

Pillows Galore

Embroidered Flower Pillow

EMBROIDERED FLOWER PILLOW

Hankie Doodle Design by Nancy Eshelman

FINISHED SIZE: 14" x 14"

FABRICS:
12" hanky with White center
¼ yard stripe for pillow front border and back

MATERIALS:
Embroidery floss
Freezer paper
Buttons
14" pillow form
1 yard of *Velcro*

CUTTING:
2 rectangles 9" x 14½" for the back
4 rectangles 2" x 15" for the mitered border

INSTRUCTIONS:

1. Back:

On one 14½" edge of each rectangle, sew a ½" hem.

Place the rectangles together, overlapping as needed to get a 14½" square.

Sew the velcro in place so it closes the overlap.

2. Front Border:

Sew the border pieces to the hanky, mitering the corners if desired.

Trim to 14½" square.

3. Embroidery and Embellishments:

Follow Basic How-Tos for transferring the design.

Embroider the flower, being careful not to drag thread across open areas on the back of the design.

Sew buttons in place as desired.

4. Pillow construction:

With right sides together, sew the back to the front all the way around.

Open the Velcro and turn the pillow right side out.

Stuff the pillow with a pillow form and close the Velcro.

Pillows Galore
see photo pages 12-13

PINK PILLOW WITH POM-POM FRINGE
Hankie Doodle Design by Nancy Eshelman
FINISHED SIZE: 15" x 15½"
FABRICS:
9" hanky with Check print
6" x 10" scrap Pink for pillow front border
¼ yard Print for outer border
½ yard White for back of pillow and backing for quilted top
MATERIALS:
Embroidery floss
Buttons
14" Pillow form
One 14" White zipper
40" White rickrack ¾" wide
16" square batting
1¾ yard Pink pom-pom fringe with 1" diameter pom-poms
CUTTING:
4 Pink rectangles 2" x 16" for the inner mitered border
4 Print rectangles 3" x 16"
INSTRUCTIONS:
1. Sew Pink border to the print border.
   Sew border to the hanky, mitering the corners.
2. Sew rickrack in place.
3. Layer lining, batting and top. Quilt as desired.
4. Sew the zipper in the back. Open the zipper.
5. Sew pom-pom trim to the back. Fold it to the inside.
6. With right sides together, sew front to back.
7. Turn right side out. Add pillow form.
8. Sew buttons in place.

YELLOW PILLOW WITH POM-POM FRINGE
Hankie Doodle Design by Nancy Eshelman
FINISHED SIZE: 15½" x 15½"
FABRICS:
9" hanky with Elephant print
½ yard Yellow for pillow top
½ yard Red for back of pillow
MATERIALS:
Embroidery floss
Buttons
14" Pillow form
60" Red rickrack 1" wide
4 Red 3" diameter yarn pom-poms
1 yard Teal pom pom fringe with ¾" diameter pom-poms
CUTTING:
15½ Yellow square
15½ Red square
INSTRUCTIONS:
1. Sew the Teal pom-pom fringe to the edge of the hanky.
2. Sew the hanky to the middle of the Yellow square.
3. Sew the rickrack to the front of the pillow.
4. With right sides together, sew the pillow back and front together, leaving an opening for stuffing.
5. Turn the pillow right side out.
6. Sew yarn pom-poms to the corners. Sew buttons in place.
7. Stuff the pillow.
8. Sew the opening closed.

RODEO PILLOW WITH POM-POM FRINGE
Hankie Doodle Design by Nancy Eshelman
FINISHED SIZE: 19" x 19"
FABRICS:
13" hanky with Rodeo print
6" x 14" scrap Red for inner border and corners
⅔ yard Blue denim for borders and back of pillow
MATERIALS:
20" Pillow form
One 18" Blue zipper
1½ yard Yellow pom-pom fringe with 1" diameter pom-poms
2¼ yard Red cording
CUTTING:
Red:
   4 squares 2½" x 2½"
   4 rectangles 1½" x 13½"
Blue:
   4 squares 1½" x 1½"
   4 rectangles 2½" x 15½"
   1 square 19" x 19" for the back of the pillow
INSTRUCTIONS:
1. Sew pom-pom fringe to the edge of the hanky.
2. Sew 2 Red rectangles to each side of the hanky.
3. Sew a Blue 1½" square to each end of 2 Red rectangles for the top and bottom borders.
4. Sew the top and bottom borders in place.
5. Sew a Blue rectangle to each side.
6. Sew a Red square to each end of 2 Blue rectangles.
7. Sew the top and bottom borders in place.
8. Sew the cording to the top of the pillow and fold to the inside.
9. Sew the zipper in the back. Open the zipper.
10. With right sides together, sew front to back.
11. Turn right side out. Add pillow form.

Rodeo Pillow Assembly Diagram

BLUE PILLOW WITH RED FRINGE

Hankie Doodle Design by Nancy Eshelman

FINISHED SIZE: 15½" x 15½"

FABRICS:
8" hanky with Bears print
½ yard Blue for pillow top and back

MATERIALS:
Embroidery floss
Buttons
14" Pillow form
1 yard Yellow ½" rickrack
1 yard Blue ¼" rickrack
60" Red fringe

CUTTING:
Two 15½ Blue squares

INSTRUCTIONS:
1. Sew the Yellow rickrack to the edge of the hanky.
2. Sew the Blue rickrack to the center of the Yellow rickrack.
3. Sew the hanky to the middle of the pillow front.
4. Sew the buttons in place.
5. Sew the fringe to the front of the pillow.
6. With right sides together, sew the pillow back and front together, leaving an opening for stuffing.
7. Turn the pillow right side out.
8. Stuff the pillow.
9. Sew the opening closed.

CHOO CHOO TRAIN PILLOW

Hankie Doodle Design by Nancy Eshelman

FINISHED SIZE: 17" x 17"

FABRICS:
12½" hanky with Check print border and White center
¼ yard Blue fabric for border and pillow back

MATERIALS:
Blue Embroidery floss
2 yards Blue cording
16" Pillow form
One 14" Blue zipper

CUTTING:
4 Blue rectangles 2" x 17" for the mitered border
1 Blue square 18" x 18" for the back

INSTRUCTIONS:
1. Follow basic instructions to transfer the drawing and embroider the train.
2. Sew border to the hanky, mitering the corners.
3. Sew cording to the pillow front.
4. Sew the zipper in the back. Open the zipper.
5. With right sides together, sew front to back.
6. Turn right side out. Add pillow form.

Under the Big Top

see photo page 14

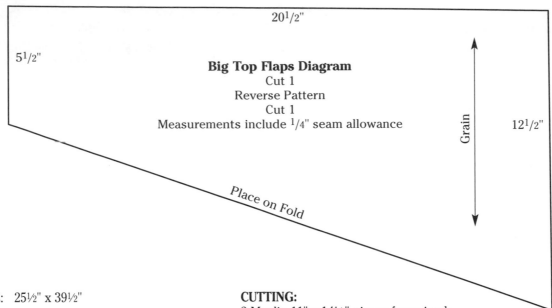

Big Top Flaps Diagram
Cut 1
Reverse Pattern
Cut 1
Measurements include 1/4" seam allowance

20½"

5½"

Grain

12½"

Place on Fold

FINISHED SIZE: 25½" x 39½"

FABRICS:
White 12" handkerchief with Black or Brown edging
⅓ yard Muslin for animal blocks
1⅔ yards Red polka dot for quilt top, binding on
     bottom edge, ties and backing
1¾ yards Stripe for valance, side curtains and
     angled top curtain
¼ yard Blue for binding three sides

MATERIALS:
Embroidery needle
Black embroidery floss
Batting
Fabric crayons
Freezer paper

CUTTING:
2 Muslin 11" x 14½" pieces for animals
Red polka dot rectangles:
     Two 3¾" x 26" for side borders
     Two 7½" x 11" for border above the muslin
     Two 5" x 11" for border below the muslin
     One 12" x 26" for the center
1 Red polka dot 2⅜" x 40" strip for bottom binding
1 Red polka dot 28" x 42" for backing
2 Red polka dot 2½" x 13½" for ties
2 Striped fabric 9" x 26" pieces for side curtains
2 Striped fabric 21" x 26" for flaps
1 Striped fabric 9" x 40" for valance
2 Blue 2⅜" x 27" strips for binding sides
1 Blue 2⅜" x 42" strips for binding top

INSTRUCTIONS:

1. Using Basic How-Tos, draw the lion and camel onto Muslin rectangles. Color with fabric crayons following manufacturer's directions. Embroider the names and around all the motifs with a Stem stitch using six strands of Black floss. Press.

2. Using Basic How-Tos, draw circus wagon onto the White hanky. Refer to the photo for placement. Embroider the wagon using 2 strands of embroidery floss. Press.

3. See Assembly Diagram. Sew 5" x 11" Polka dot rectangle to the bottom of each Muslin rectangle.
     Sew the 7½" x 11 Polka dot rectangles to the top. Press.
     Sew the 12" x 26" Polka dot rectangle between the Muslin rectangles.
     Sew a 3¾" x 26" Polka dot rectangle to the sides. Press.

4. Position the embroidered hanky in the middle and Blind Hem stitch it in place. See photo.

5. Layer backing, batting and top. Baste. Quilt. Trim backing and batting to the quilt top.

6. Fold Red polka dot binding strip in half lengthwise wrong sides together. Press. Sew to the bottom edge of quilt. Turn to back and bind.

7. Fold one 9" x 26" Stripe in half lengthwise with right sides together and sew across one short end. Turn right side out. Press. Place on top of the side of the quilt, raw edges together, and the hem even with the bottom. Pin and sew. Repeat for the other side. Bind both sides with Blue following Step 6.

8. Place the pattern for the top flaps on Striped 21" x 26" fabric at fold and cut one out. Reverse the pattern and cut out another. Fold Striped top curtain in half with right sides together. Sew across the 2 ends. Turn right side out. Repeat for the other side. Press. Place flaps across the top edge of the quilt with raw edges together. Make sure the side with the stripes at an angle faces to the front. (See photo.) Pin. Sew.

9. Fold Striped valance in half with right sides together. Sew across the two ends. Turn right side out. Press. Place across the top edge of quilt with raw edges together. Pin and sew. Bind top edge with Blue strip following instructions in step 6.

10. Ties: With wrong sides together, fold the Red polka dot piece lengthwise. Pin and sew long seam. Turn right side out. Fold raw edges at ends to the inside to form a slight angle. Stitch. Tie strip into a loose half knot. Hand-stitch to the curtain. Repeat for the other side.

Big Top Quilt Assembly Diagram

7" x 10½"	11½" x 25½"	7" x 10½"
10½" x 14"		10½" x 14"
3¼" x 25½"	Circus Wagon	3¼" x 25½"
4½" x 10½"		4½" x 10½"

25½" x 39½"

CIRCUS

HUMPY

KING

Fancy Framed Handkerchief

see photo page 15

designed by Janice Beals

Special handkerchiefs deserve special framing. The stenciled leaf is the perfect complement for this beautiful handkerchief.

Want a tidy, tasteful, trendy, treasure? Try this terrific tray. I found a fabulous vintage hanky, but the hem was tattered, so I sewed a narrow picot ribbon to cover it.

It's a good idea to make friends with your neighborhood framer. This project is much easier if you can charm the framer into finishing the assembly for you!

FINISHED SIZE: 23½" x 24½"

MATERIALS:
Handkerchief with a wide border or solid color outer edge
Matboard cut to size
Prismacolor colored pencils
Transfer paper
Frame

INSTRUCTIONS:
1. Measure handkerchief.

Add 4" to all four sides for outside dimensions of matboard.

Subtract ¾" from the width and ¾" from the length of the handkerchief for the inside opening of the matboard. This allows the matboard to cover the attached edge of the hanky.

Have a framer cut the mat to the correct dimensions for your handkerchief.

2. See photo for placement of the pattern on matboard.

Place transfer paper on the matboard and the pattern on top of it.

Outline each design with its basic color. Fill with color. Add shadow outline for emphasis if desired.

3. Take mat to framer. Choose frame to coordinate. Have framer finish project.

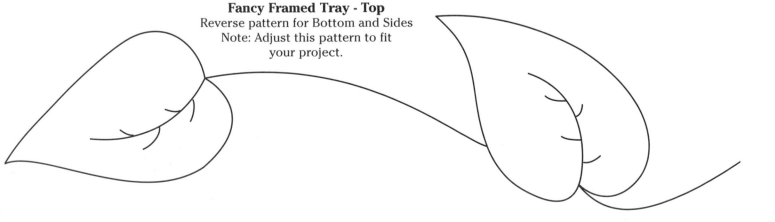

Fancy Framed Tray - Top
Reverse pattern for Bottom and Sides
Note: Adjust this pattern to fit
your project.

by Janice Beals

FINISHED SIZE: 16" x 24½"

MATERIALS:

Handkerchief

2 Vintage hand towels or a dresser scarf with beautiful decorative ends

1½ yards Satin ribbon 1½" wide for handle ties

1½ yards Picot ribbon to cover edge of handkerchief, if needed

Picture Frame

Matboard in coordinating color

Glass to fit

1 cardboard backing

"Spacers"

Tiny nails

4 eye screws – large enough to feed 1½" ribbon through but not so large they split the frame when attached

4 Wood ½" candle cups with a hole in the bottom for tray feet

4 Screws to attach the wood feet

White paint

White paper as large as frame

Double-stick tape

INSTRUCTIONS:

1. Plan the layout of the handkerchief/towel design before purchasing the frame and frame supplies.
   a. Lay hand towels flat and center the handkerchief on top.
   b. Adjust the amount towels show beyond the handkerchief as desired.
   c. At the left edge of the handkerchief, mark the towels where they overlap.
   d. Add ¼" to each towel beyond this mark.
   e. Cut off the towels at this line. Sew the towels together using ¼" seam. Press.
   f. Center handkerchief on sewn towels. Sew handkerchief to towels.
2. Take the sewn handkerchief to the frame store.
   Purchase the frame and framing supplies.
3. Attach eye screws 4" apart on opposite sides of the frame.
4. Attach wood feet to the bottom of the frame at each corner using screws.
5. Paint the entire piece White.
6. Return project to the framer to finish the assembly or proceed to step 7.
7. Place the handkerchief/towels on top of the matboard.
   Place the glass on top of the handkerchief. Place frame on top of glass.
   Holding everything together tightly, turn the frame upside down.
   If hanky "bubbles", place spacers between glass and hanky.
   If needed, tape towels along the outside edges to hold them in place.
8. Position cardboard backing.
   Use tiny nails around the edge spaced every few inches apart to secure.
9. Cut White paper just a smidge smaller than the frame.
   Cut paper around the feet so that it lies flat.
   Apply double-stick tape around the edge of the frame and press the White paper onto it.
10. Cut 1½" ribbon in half.
    Thread ribbon through the eye screws and tie into a bow.
    Repeat for the other side.

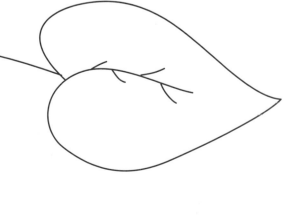

Butterfly Quilt

see photo page 16

designed by Karin Goudy

FINISHED SIZE: 65" x 78"

FABRICS:

16 Handkerchiefs for butterflies

6 yards White on White print for blocks and borders

⅔ yard Yellows each of six assorted prints for lilies, buds and prairie points

1⅔ yards Green for vines and leaves

⅛ yard Dark Brown for butterfly heads

2⅜ yards White 90" wide for backing

Scraps of Red, Yellow, Dark Brown and Medium Brown for hummingbird

Batting

MATERIALS:

Embroidery floss to match Green fabric

DMC embroidery floss (#335 Pink for daylily stamen, #961 Brown for butterfly antenna)

Embroidery floss coordinating with butterfly handkerchiefs to applique

Embroidery needle size 8

Applique needle size 11 sharp

CUTTING:

16 White 14½" x 14½" squares for butterfly blocks

2 White 7" x 26½" for inner border

2 White 7" x 39½" for inner border

2 White 7" x 65½" for outer border

2 White 7" x 78½" for outer border

Green 40" x 40" square for 500" bias cut 1¼" wide

18 Yellow 4¼" x 4¼" squares out of each Yellow fabric for 106 prairie points

INSTRUCTIONS:

1. Butterfly squares:
   a. Fold hanky following diagrams on pages 88-89.
      Pin onto White square.
   b. Applique with coordinating thread using a Blanket stitch.
   c. Add ³⁄₁₆" seam allowance to the head pattern.
      Cut out and sew in place using the Needle Turn Applique stitch.
      Embroider antenna with Stem stitch.
      Repeat for all 16 blocks.
   d. Press. Trim blocks to 13½" x 13½".
2. See photo for the placement of butterflies as you sew the top together.
3. Sew 2 butterfly blocks together for the center.
   Sew the inner border strips in place. Press. Miter the corners.
4. Sew 2 butterfly blocks together and then sew them to the top border.
   Repeat for the bottom border. Press.
5. Sew 4 butterfly blocks together in a column.
   Sew onto the left side of the inner border. Repeat for the right side. Press.
6. Sew the outer border strips in place. Press. Miter corners.
7. Fold bias in half wrong sides together. Press. Lay it around the inner border forming the vine. See photo.
   Pin. Sew it on using ¼" seam allowance. Bend the folded edge over the seam, encasing the raw edge.
      Stitch it down by hand.
8. Cut out leaves, day lilies, buds and petals, adding ³⁄₁₆" seam allowances to patterns.
   See photo for placement and stitch in place.
   Add embroidery tendrils to the vines and stamens to the day lilies.
9. Repeat step 6 and 7 for the outer border.
10. Cut out hummingbird pieces, adding ³⁄₁₆" seam allowance to the pattern.
    See photo for placement on the inner border and stitch in place.
    Add eye and beak with Satin stitch embroidery.

11. Layer, backing, batting and top to form a sandwich. Baste layers together. Quilt as desired, leaving room to fold the back of the quilt out of the way for the prairie points.
    Trim the backing and batting to the edge of the quilt top.
12. Fold the back of the quilt out of the way. Place the prairie points on top of the quilt along the edge.
    Sew the prairie points to the top through the batting. Fold the points up, turning the seam to the inside.
    Turn the seam allowance under on the back. Sew it down by hand using a Blanket stitch.

Instructions for Attaching Bias Vine

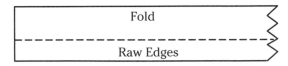

Extend to desired length. →

Cut on bias 1¹⁄₄" wide.

Fold

Raw Edges

Fold bias in half and press.

Fold

Raw Edges

Position on quilt top. Machine stitch to top using ¹⁄₄" seam.

Machine stitched side.

Hand stitched side.

Flip folded side down across the seam allowance, encasing it and hand stitch it in place using a blind hem stitch.

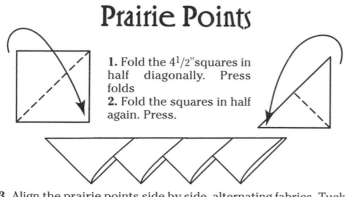

Prairie Points

1. Fold the $4^1/2$" squares in half diagonally. Press folds

2. Fold the squares in half again. Press.

3. Align the prairie points side by side, alternating fabrics. Tuck one end of the point inside the open edge of the next point.

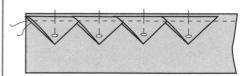

Fold the back of the quilt out of the way. Sew the prairie points to the top of the quilt.

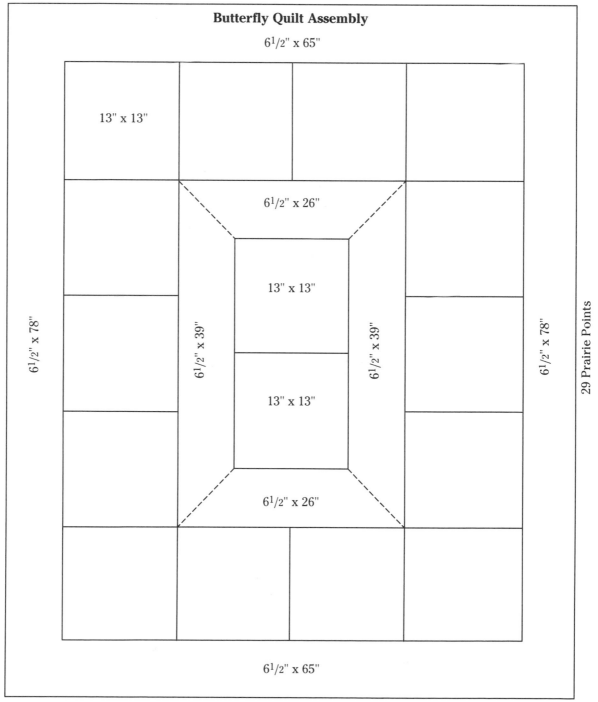

Butterfly Quilt Assembly

$6^1/2$" x 65"

13" x 13"

$6^1/2$" x 26"

$6^1/2$" x 78"

$6^1/2$" x 39"

13" x 13"

$6^1/2$" x 39"

13" x 13"

$6^1/2$" x 78"

$6^1/2$" x 26"

$6^1/2$" x 65"

29 Prairie Points

24 Prairie Points

Butterfly Quilt
see photo page 16

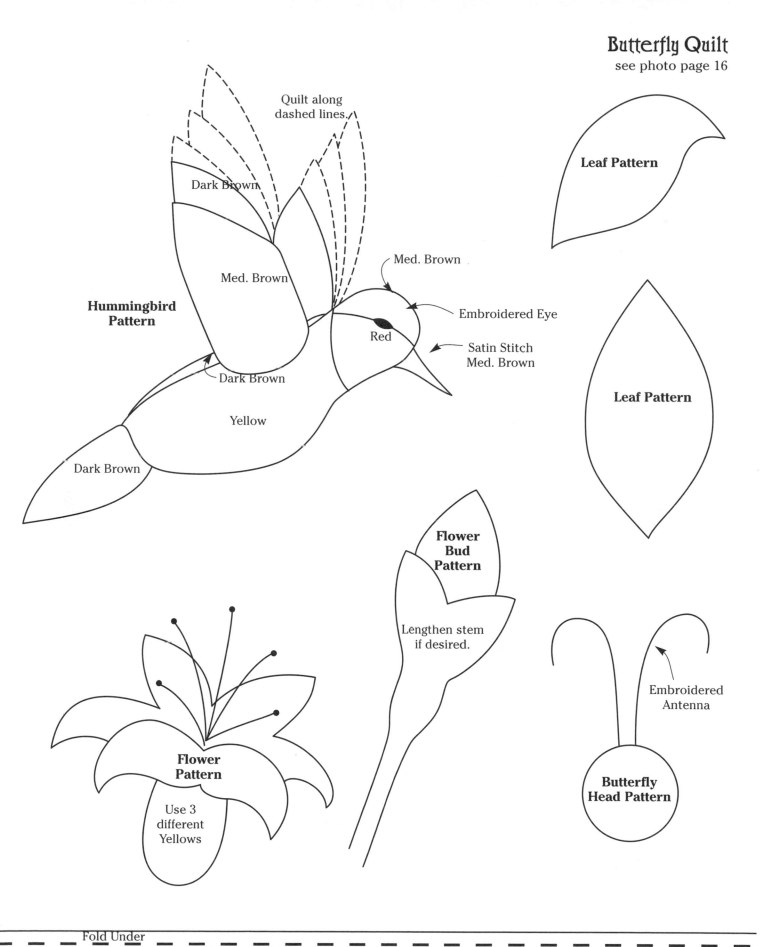

Butterfly Quilt
see photo page 16

Quilt along
dashed lines.

Leaf Pattern

Dark Brown

Med. Brown

Med. Brown

**Hummingbird
Pattern**

Embroidered Eye

Satin Stitch
Med. Brown

Red

Dark Brown

Yellow

Leaf Pattern

Dark Brown

**Flower
Bud
Pattern**

Lengthen stem
if desired.

Embroidered
Antenna

**Flower
Pattern**

Use 3
different
Yellows

**Butterfly
Head Pattern**

- - - Fold Under - - -

Butterfly Vine Applique Pattern

- - - Fold Under - - -

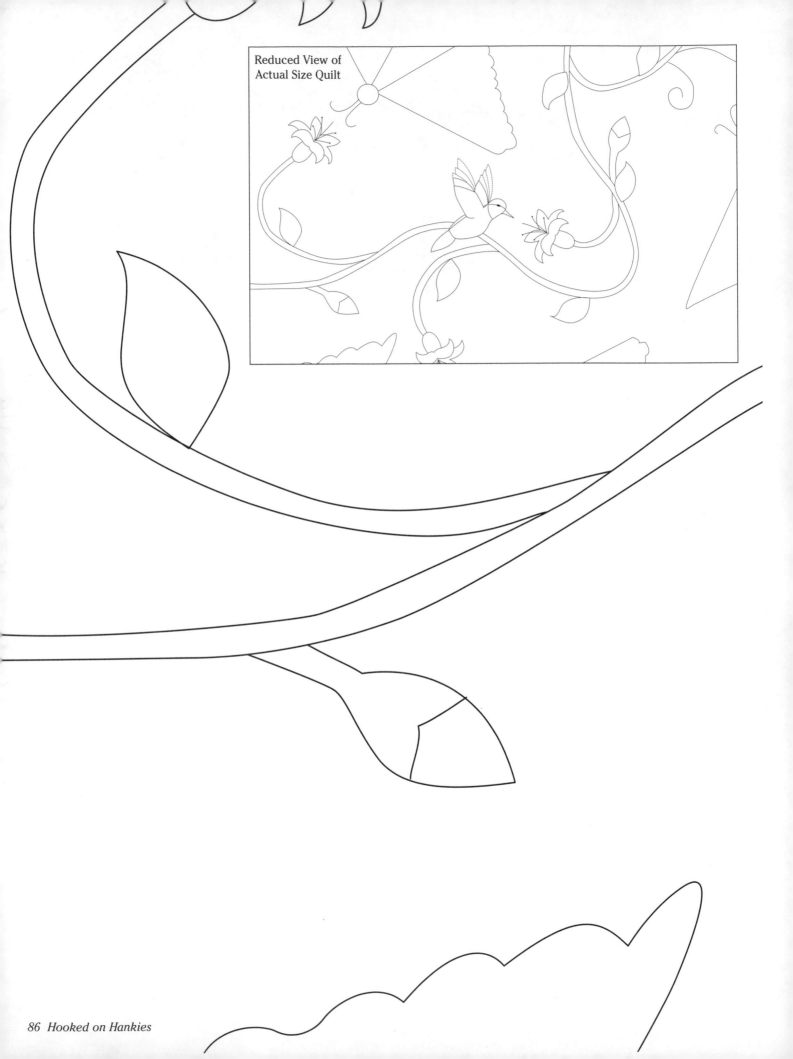

Reduced View of
Actual Size Quilt

Actual Size Quilt Patterns
showing how vine, leaves, buds and
flowers are placed and stitched on quilt.

Butterfly Quilt
see photo page 16

Folding the Butterfly Hanky Body

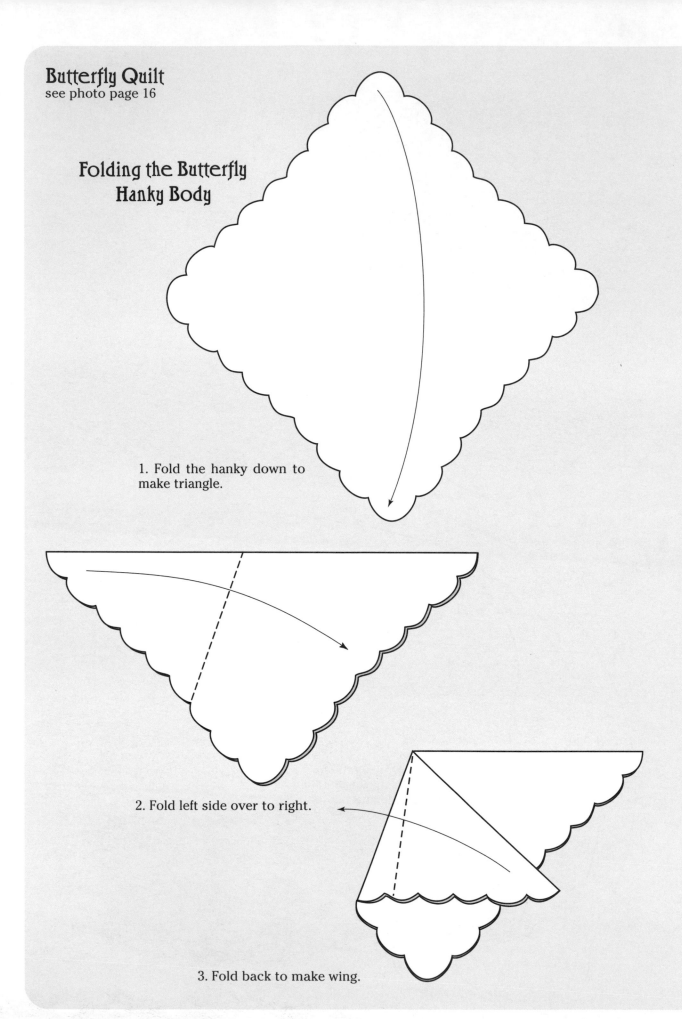

1. Fold the hanky down to make triangle.

2. Fold left side over to right.

3. Fold back to make wing.

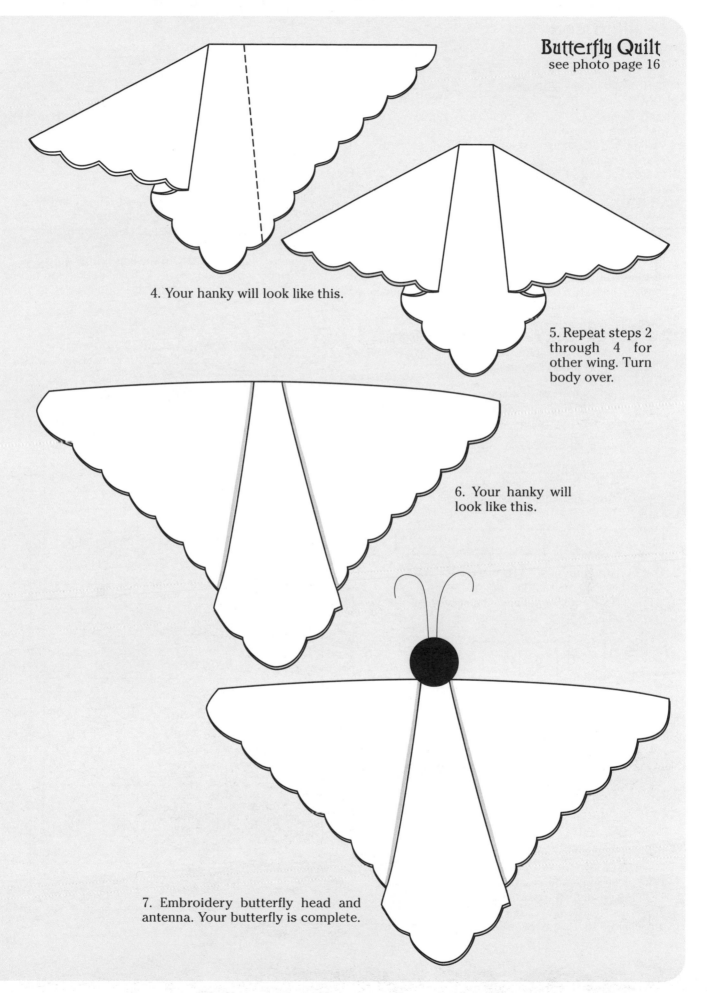

4. Your hanky will look like this.

5. Repeat steps 2 through 4 for other wing. Turn body over.

6. Your hanky will look like this.

7. Embroidery butterfly head and antenna. Your butterfly is complete.

Chenille Throw

see photo page 17

FINISHED SIZE: 54" x 82"

FABRICS:

8 Handkerchiefs 12½" x 12½" from hanky yardage
1 yard Green for sashing
⅛ yard or 5" x 10" scrap Pink for corner squares
2⅓ yards Chenille
2⅜ yards Backing 60" wide
Batting

MATERIALS:

7¾ yards fringe

CUTTING:

2 Chenille 5½" x 82½" for side borders
2 Chenille 5½" x 44½" for top and bottom borders
7 Chenille 12½" x 12½" squares
8 handkerchiefs 12½" x 12½" squares cut from hankie yardage
22 Green 2½" x 12½" strips for sashing
2 Green 2½" x 40½" strips for top and bottom sashing
2 Green 2½" x 72½" strips for left and right side sashing
8 Pink 2½" x 2½" squares for sashing corners

INSTRUCTIONS:

1. Horizontal Sashing: Make 4 of these.

Sew a Green 2½" x 12½" sashing piece to a 2½" Pink square. Press. Make 2. Sew them together.

Sew a Green 2½" x 12½" sashing piece to the end of the strip.

2. Row Construction: Make 3 Handkerchief rows.

Sew these together in this order:

12½" Handkerchief square, Green sashing 2½" x 12½", Chenille square, Green sashing, Handkerchief square.

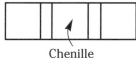

Chenille

3. Row Construction: Make 2 Chenille rows.

Sew these together in this order:

12½" Chenille square, Green sashing 2½" x 12½", Handkerchief square, Green sashing, Chenille square.

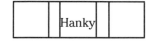

Hanky

4. Horizontal Sashings:

Sew a horizontal sashing strip from Step 1 to the bottom of 2 Handkerchief rows and 2 Chenille rows.

One Handkerchief row will not get a sashing strip.

5. Top Construction:

Assemble the rows according to the diagram and

photo.

6. Top and Bottom Sashing:

Sew the Green 2½" x 40½" sashing strips to the top and bottom. Press.

7. Side Sashing:

Sew the Green side sashing strips to the left and right side. Press.

8. Chenille Borders:

Sew Chenille top and bottom borders to the quilt. Press.
Sew Chenille side borders to the quilt. Press.

9. Layer backing, batting, and top to form a sandwich. Baste the layers together. Quilt as desired.

10. Trim the backing and batting to the edge of the quilt top.

11. Turn Chenille and backing edges into each other and topstitch.

12. Overlap the quilt edge with the fringe and topstitch in place.

Chenille Throw Assembly Diagram

5" x 44"		
2" x 40"		
12" x 12" Hanky	Chenille	Hanky
2" x 12"	P	P
Chenille	Hanky	Chenille
	P	P
Hanky	Chenille	Hanky
	P	P
Chenille	Hanky	Chenille
	P	P
Hanky	Chenille	Hanky

5" x 82"   2" x 72"

HANKY DOLLS

FINISHED SIZE: 8"

MATERIALS:

Handkerchief - at least 9" x 9"

4" Pregathered lace

½ yard Satin ribbon ¼" wide

Crochet thread in coordinating color

Handful of stuffing – even a few cotton balls will work

INSTRUCTIONS:

1. Head: Place a small amount of stuffing just off center of the handkerchief and pull the hankie around it to form the head. Wrap crochet thread around the base of the stuffing to make the neck. Tie the threads and trim the ends.

2. Arms: Form another ball of stuffing using about ¾ of the amount used for the head. Place it just below the head and slightly toward the back of the hanky. Tie.

Repeat for the other arm.

Placement of these arms is a little tricky. You'll have to work with these a bit to ensure the arms are the same size and close to the head. It is better if the arms flop forward instead of back. Also, stuffing needs to be somewhat fluffy.

3. Squeeze a small amount of the arm, including stuffing, and tie off to form a tiny hand.

Repeat for the other arm.

4. Center lace on the ribbon. Stitch lace to the ribbon. Place it around the head and tie it underneath making a bonnet. Stitch to the head if desired.

FOLDED PINCUSHION OR SACHET

Hankie Doodle Design by Nancy Eshelman

FINISHED SIZE: 4½" x 4½"

FABRICS:

10" x 10" handkerchief with lace edging

MATERIALS:

Stuffing

Embellishments as desired

INSTRUCTIONS:

1. Fold handkerchief in half. Sew sides together ¼" to ½" below the lace.

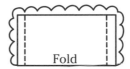

2. Refold handkerchief so the two unsewn edges are together. Sew this side together following directions in step 1. Leave 3" unsewn at one end to allow room for stuffing.

3. Position the handkerchief points so they come together in the middle of the small square like the diagram. Stuff sachet lightly through the opening. Sew opening closed.

4. Do a Tacking stitch from the back through the handkerchief to the center front where all the points come together. Pull thread tight and tie off. This makes the top of the cushion sink down,

5. Embellish with buttons or other trim as desired.

Making the Hanky Doll

1. Make head.

2. Make arm.

3. Make hand.

Repeat for other arm and hand.

4. Make bonnet.

Tie ribbon underneath head.

Embroidery Stitches

Working with Floss.
Separate embroidery floss. Use 24" lengths of floss and a #8 embroidery needle. Use 1 or 2 strands unless otherwise directed.

Pay attention to backgrounds.

When working with lighter-colored fabrics, do not carry dark flosses across large unworked background areas. Stop and start again to prevent unsightly 'ghost strings' from showing through the front.

Another option is to back tinted muslin with another layer of muslin before adding embroidery stitches. This helps keep 'ghost strings' from showing.

Blanket Stitch

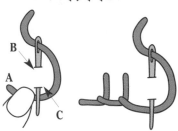

Come up at A, hold the thread down with your thumb, go down at B. Come back up at C with the needle tip over the thread. Pull the stitch into place. Repeat, outlining with the bottom legs of the stitch. Use this stitch to edge fabrics.

Chain Stitch

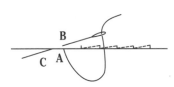

Come up at A. To form a loop, hold the thread down with your thumb, go down at B (as close as possible to A). Come back up at C with the needle tip over the thread. Repeat to form a chain.

Needle Turn Applique

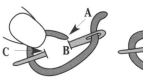

Come out through the fold of the applique fabric. Place the needle point just under the edge of the folded fabric and come up a short distance away through the fold again.

French Knot

Come up at A. Wrap the floss around the needle 2 to 3 times. Insert the needle close to A. Hold the floss and pull the needle through the loops gently.

Backstitch (Outline Stitch)

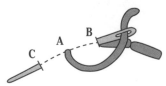

Come up at A, go down at B. Come back up at C. Repeat.

Running Stitch

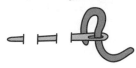

Come up at A. Weave the needle through the fabric, making short, even stitches. Use this stitch to gather fabrics, too.

Satin Stitch

Work small straight stitches close together and at the same angle to fill an area with stitches. Vary the length of the stitches as required to keep the outline of the area smooth.

Stem Stitch

Work from left to right to make regular, slanting stitches along the stitch line. Bring the needle up above the center of the last stitch.

Straight Stitch

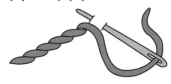

Come up at A and go down at B to form a simple flat stitch. Use this stitch for hair for animals and for simple petals on small flowers.

Whip Stitch

Insert the needle under a few fibers of one layer of fabric. Bring the needle up through the other layer of fabric. Use this stitch to attach the folded raw edges of fabric to the back of pieces or to attach bindings around the edges of quilts and coverlets.

Helpful Hint

To make sharp, clean corners, come up at A, go down at B. Come up at C (at corner) with needle tip over thread. Go down at D to secure loop at corner, come back up at B.

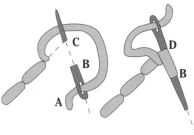

PAUSE... TAKE A BREAK

FINISHED SIZE: 24½" x 23"

FABRIC:

3 different 12" hankies

¼ yard Light Blue on White print background for cups

⅓ yard of 2 different Light Blue prints for pot backgrounds

¼ yard Blue print for large coffee pot

¼ yard Blue print for smaller teapot

⅛ yard Blue check for mugs

⅛ yard Dark Blue print for cup and saucer

½ yard Dark Blue print for sashings, borders and binding

⅔ yard Light Blue print for backing

MATERIALS:

Applique needle size 11 sharp

Batting

CUTTING:

2 hankies cut in half diagonally.

    You will have one half left over from each hanky.

Cut off the corners from the other hanky using the

    corner pattern.

Top rectangle 8" x 22" for cups

Left rectangle 11" x 13" for coffee pot

Right rectangle 11" x 13" for teapot

1 Dark Blue 2" x 12¼ for vertical sashing

1 Dark Blue 2" x 21½ for horizontal sashing

2 Dark Blue 2" x 23" for side borders

2 Dark Blue 2" x 21½" for top and bottom borders

Backing and batting 24" x 26"

3 Dark Blue 2½" x 44 sewn together for 100" binding

INSTRUCTIONS:

1. Place 1 handkerchief half on the coffee pot rectangle so the hanky's raw edge is 4¾" above the bottom edge.

    Place the other hanky half on the teapot rectangle so the raw edge is 5½" above the bottom edge.

    Turn the raw edges under ¼". Pin. Applique this edge to the rectangle using the needle turn applique stitch.

    The two hemmed sides of the hanky are left unsewn.

2. Cut out the coffee and teapot adding a ⅛" seam allowance. Pin in place and Needle Turn Applique. Press.

    Fold the bottom of the hankies out of the way and trim an equal amount from all sides to measure 10¼" x 12¼".

3. Sew 3 hanky triangles into a long strip by joining them at the seam line marked on the pattern.

4. Lay this 3-hanky group across the top rectangle 3" from the bottom edge. Turn under the long raw edge ¼".

    Pin. Applique. The hemmed sides of the hankies are left unsewn.

5. Cut out mugs, teacup and saucer, adding a ⅛" seam allowance. See photo for positioning on the top rectangle.

    Pin. Applique. Press.

6. Fold the bottoms of the hankies out of the way and trim top rectangle to 6¾" x 21½".

7. Sew a Dark Blue 2" x 12¼" strip between the coffee pot and teapot blocks. Press.

    Sew a Dark Blue 2" x 21½" strip to the top of the pot section.

    Sew this to the bottom of the cup section. Press.

8. Sew a Dark Blue 2" x 21½" border strip to the top and bottom of the wall hanging. Press.

9. Sew a Dark Blue 2" x 23" border strip to the sides of the wall hanging. Press.

10. Layer backing, batting and top to form a sandwich. Baste layers together. Quilt as desired.

    Trim the backing and batting to the edge of the quilt top.

11. Sew binding to make a 100" long strip. Press binding in half lengthwise. Use ⅜" or ¼" seam allowance and sew binding to the quilt front. Turn to back. Hem by hand.

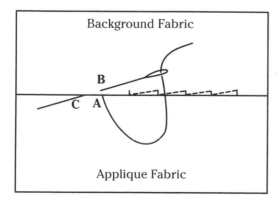

Dashed line is the thread
under both fabrics.

Needle Turn Applique Stitch

Place the applique piece onto the background fabric. Pin or baste in place. Along a straight section, turn the seam allowance under. Bring the needle out through the edge of the fold of the applique at A. Straight across from this and slightly under the appliqued edge, put the needle down through the background fabric to the back B. Bring the needle up a short distance away through the fold of the applique again at C and continue stitching. Use the needle to roll the seam allowance under about 1/2" ahead of your stitching. If this is done properly, the stitches are so small that no thread will show.

Pause... Take a Break

see photo page 99

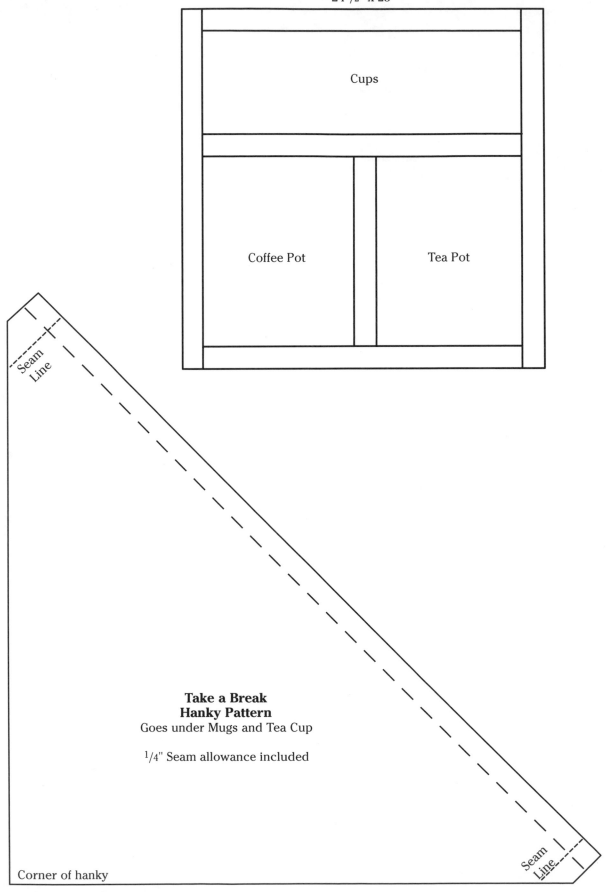

Take a Break Assembly Diagram

$24^1/2$" x 23"

Cups

Coffee Pot

Tea Pot

Seam
Line

**Take a Break
Hanky Pattern**
Goes under Mugs and Tea Cup

$1/4$" Seam allowance included

Corner of hanky

Seam
Line

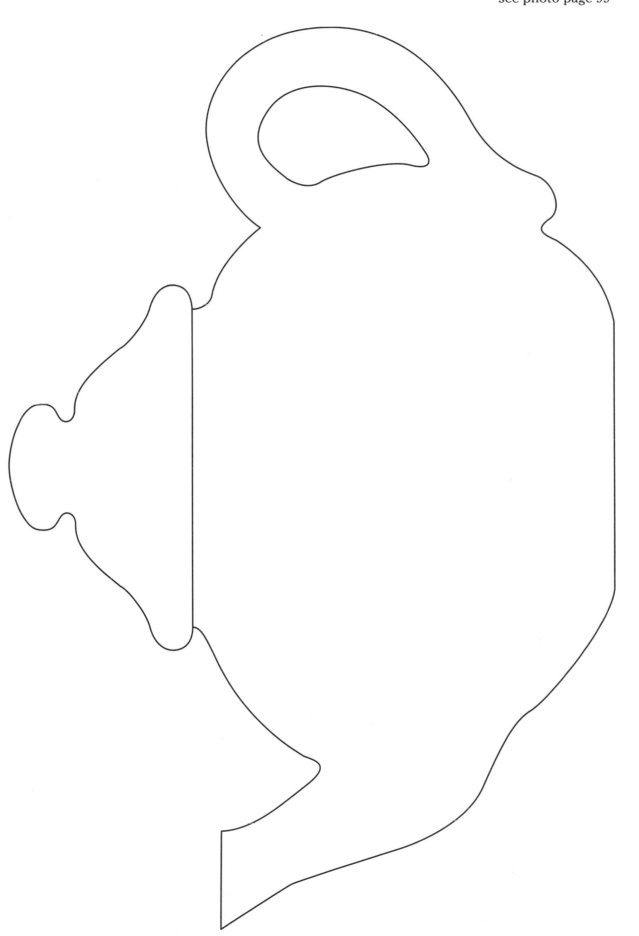

Many thanks to those whose wonderful skills are on display in this book:

Doretha Albee
Gwen Albert
Betty Alderman
Janice Beals
Anna Boyer
Jeanne Bradbury
Cindy Chapin
Denise Domino
Diane Ebner
Diane P. Edwards
Nancy Eshelman
Kim Gammill
Joe Goldwater
Karin Goudy
Joan Hahn
Patty Harvey
Nola Heidbreder
Mary Andra Holmes
Kay Hunzinger
Betty Isbel
DiAnn Iverson
Una Jarvis
Helen Johnston
Dee Lynn
Carol Meka
Lynnette Mault
Cindy Taylor Oates
Helen Ohlson
Donna Olson
Diane Pitchford
Nancy Shamy
Frances Smith
Arlene Southworth
Terri Steimel
Sandra Streech
Fran Techlow
Audrey Waite,
Shirley Weagant
A.J. Wischmeyer
Jude Vegso

MANY THANKS to my friends for their cheerful help and wonderful ideas!
Kathy McMillan
Jennifer Laughlin
Patty Williams
Marti Wyble
Janie Ray • Donna Kinsey
David & Donna Thomason

Pause... Take a Break
see photo on page 99

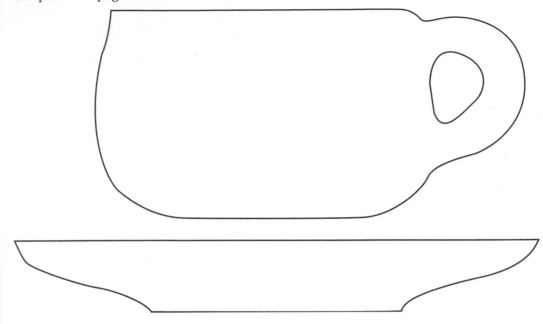

Knowing this makes working with handkerchiefs easier:

1. Most old handkerchiefs are not square. They are usually slightly rectangular. Always measure both sides of every hanky.

2. Old handkerchiefs are delicate. They will not hold up for much washing. Choose new hanky yardage for projects that will receive heavy use.

3. Most handkerchiefs have poorly sewn corners. The exact point may have actually come unstitched or not be sewn straight. I did a lot of corner repair.

4. It often takes more hankies than estimated because some of the corners are not usable. Old hankies may also have a hole or damage that doesn't show up until you start to cut into them. So always plan for extra hankies.

5. Many handkerchiefs have a design or narrow contrasting color along their edge, which makes them prettier to applique onto a background instead of sewing borders onto them.

6. Press each handkerchief with spray sizing or starch to stabilize it before working with it.

7. Lightweight fusible interfacing can also be used to stabilize. If the edge of the handkerchief is scalloped, make sure to cut the stabilizer smaller so that it will not stick out anywhere along the irregular edge.

8. Vintage cocktail or ultra small dinner napkins of the past are also great to use in these projects.

9. Soaking handkerchiefs that are dingy, stained, or any shade of White with OxiClean will make them as beautiful as possible. I fell in love with the results that this product achieves.

10. If the handkerchief hem has a rolled edge, applique it with a Blind Hem stitch. If handkerchief hem is Satin stitched, applique it with a Tacking stitch.

To adapt designs on hankies for embroidery motifs:

1. Select a motif from the hanky that you like.

2. Place tracing paper on top of the hanky and trace the motif with a pencil.

3. Go over the line drawing with an ink pen to clean up the lines and darken the image.

4. Enlarge or reduce the design with a copy machine until the size is perfect.

5. Follow the Basic How-Tos on page 99 for transferring the design to fabric.